# The Republic

BY

## Jane Yarbrough
Instructor
Wisconsin Center—Marinette

**BARRON'S**

BARRON'S EDUCATIONAL SERIES, INC.
Woodbury, New York

*To my philosophy students
at the University of Wisconsin
Center—Marinette.*

## ACKNOWLEDGMENTS

We would like to acknowledge the many painstaking hours of work
Holly Hughes and Thomas F. Hirsch have devoted to making the
*Book Notes* series a success.

© Copyright 1984 by Barron's Educational Series, Inc.

All rights reserved.
No part of this book may be reproduced
by photostat, microfilm, xerography
means, or incorporated into any i
system, electronic or mechanica
permission of the copyright ov

*All inquiries should be addressed to:*
Barron's Educational Series, Inc.
113 Crossways Park Drive
Woodbury, New York 11797

*Library of Congress Catalog Card No. 84-18456*

International Standard Book No. 0-8120-3436-8

**Library of Congress Cataloging in Publication Data**
Yarbrough, Jane.
  Plato's The republic.

  (Barron's book notes)
  Bibliography: p. 123
  Summary: A guide to reading "The Republic" with a
critical and appreciative mind. Includes background on
the author's life and times, sample tests, term paper
suggestions, and a reading list.
    1. Plato. Republic. [1. Plato. Republic.
2. Classical literature—History and criticism]
I. Title. II. Series.
JC71.P6Y37  1984    321'.07     84-18456
ISBN 0-8120-3436-8 (pbk.)

PRINTED IN THE UNITED STATES OF AMERICA

456     550     987654321

# CONTENTS

Advisory Board   v

How to Use This Book   vii

**THE AUTHOR AND HIS TIMES**   1

**THE BOOK**   5

Some Basics About the Book   5

Socrates as a Character   6

Form and Style   8

**The Dialogue**   10

**A STEP BEYOND**   105

Tests and Answers   105

Term Paper Ideas   121

Further Reading   123

    Critical Works   123

    Selected Translations of

    *The Republic*   123

    Author's Selected Works   124

Glossary   127

The Critics   131

# ADVISORY BOARD

We wish to thank the following educators who helped us focus our *Book Notes* series to meet student needs and critiqued our manuscripts to provide quality materials.

Murray Bromberg, Principal
Wang High School of Queens, Holliswood, New York

Sandra Dunn, English Teacher
Hempstead High School, Hempstead, New York

Lawrence J. Epstein, Associate Professor of English
Suffolk County Community College, Selden, New York

Leonard Gardner, Lecturer, English Department
State University of New York at Stony Brook

Beverly A. Haley, Member, Advisory Committee
National Council of Teachers of English Student
Guide Series, Fort Morgan, Colorado

Elaine C. Johnson, English Teacher
Tamalpais Union High School District
Mill Valley, California

Marvin J. LaHood, Professor of English
State University of New York College at Buffalo

Robert Lecker, Associate Professor of English
McGill University, Montréal, Québec, Canada

David E. Manly, Professor of Educational Studies
State University of New York College at Geneseo

Bruce Miller, Associate Professor of Education
State University of New York at Buffalo

Frank O'Hare, Professor of English
Ohio State University, Columbus, Ohio

Faith Z. Schullstrom, Member, Executive Committee
National Council of Teachers of English
Director of Curriculum and Instruction
Guilderland Central School District, New York

Mattie C. Williams, Director, Bureau of Language Arts
Chicago Public Schools, Chicago, Illinois

# HOW TO USE THIS BOOK

You have to know how to approach literature in order to get the most out of it. This *Barron's Book Notes* volume follows a plan based on methods used by some of the best students to read a work of literature.

Begin with the guide's section on the author's life and times. As you read, try to form a clear picture of the author's personality, circumstances, and motives for writing the work. This background usually will make it easier for you to hear the author's tone of voice, and follow where the author is heading.

Then go over the rest of the introductory material—such sections as those on the plot, characters, setting, themes, and style of the work. Underline, or write down in your notebook, particular things to watch for, such as contrasts between characters and repeated literary devices. At this point, you may want to develop a system of symbols to use in marking your text as you read. (Of course, you should only mark up a book you own, not one that belongs to another person or a school.) Perhaps you will want to use a different letter for each character's name, a different number for each major theme of the book, a different color for each important symbol or literary device. Be prepared to mark up the pages of your book as you read. Put your marks in the margins so you can find them again easily.

Now comes the moment you've been waiting for—the time to start reading the work of literature. You may want to put aside your *Barron's Book Notes* volume until you've read the work all the way through. Or you may want to alternate, reading the *Book Notes* analysis of each section as soon as you have finished reading the corresponding part of the original. Before you move on, reread crucial passages you don't fully understand. (Don't take this guide's analysis for granted—make up your own mind as to what the work means.)

Once you've finished the whole work of literature, you may want to review it right away, so you can firm up your ideas about what it means. You may want to leaf through the book concentrating on passages you marked in reference to one character or one theme. This is also a good time to reread the *Book Notes* introductory material, which pulls together insights on specific topics.

When it comes time to prepare for a test or to write a paper, you'll already have formed ideas about the work. You'll be able to go back through it, refreshing your memory as to the author's exact words and perspective, so that you can support your opinions with evidence drawn straight from the work. Patterns will emerge, and ideas will fall into place; your essay question or term paper will almost write itself. Give yourself a dry run with one of the sample tests in the guide. These tests present both multiple-choice and essay questions. An accompanying section gives answers to the multiple-choice questions as well as suggestions for writing the essays. If you have to select a term paper topic, you may choose one from the list of suggestions in this book. This guide also provides you with a reading list, to help you when you start research for a term paper, and a selection of provocative comments by critics, to spark your thinking before you write.

# THE AUTHOR AND HIS TIMES

The man called Plato who wrote *The Republic* grew up in the Greek city-state of Athens during the tragic decline of that glorious civilization. Born about 427 B.C., Plato was the son of one of Athens' aristocratic families and the descendant of kings. His real name was Aristocles. "Plato" is a Greek nickname meaning "broad."

A year or so before Plato's birth, Pericles—the great statesman and democratic leader of Athens—died, leaving behind a reign that had fostered superb artistic achievements in architecture, sculpture, and literature and brilliant accomplishments in history and science. But Pericles also left behind a war between democratic Athens and Sparta, a nearby Greek city-state ruled by a military elite. This conflict for economic and ideological dominance, known as the Peloponnesian War (431–404 B.C.), ended in the defeat of Athens and brought to a close the Golden Age that Athens had known under Pericles' leadership.

Before their defeat the Athenians had thought that they were the most splendid of people, living as they did in a society devoted to intellectual and cultural pursuits, a democracy in which every male citizen had a voice in governmental policy (the many slaves in Athens—the human spoils of war—had no political voice, nor did women). The defeat by Sparta brought the Athenians to their financial knees, wounded their considerable pride, and caused them to distrust their social and political institutions.

At this time Plato was twenty-three years old and was disillusioned with the Athenian democratic government and the traditional form of Athenian education. Plato probably fought in the Peloponnesian War. Returning from war defeated, with hopes dashed for the continuation of a prosperous, powerful government, Plato turned to ideas on social and political reform. If times had been different he might have become a financier, a politician, or both. Instead he met Socrates, and with Socrates as his mentor, Plato became a philosopher.

The word *philosophy* comes from the Greek language and means "the love of wisdom." Socrates was a lover of wisdom, a seeker of truth. His primary mission, as revealed in Plato's writings, was to discover that which is true and good about human nature. He stalked the streets of Athens questioning the prominent citizens on their beliefs. He found that few people, including himself, knew much about what it was to live the Good Life. And he let the citizens know that he knew that they didn't really know what they were talking about, that their convictions were not based on sound logic. This behavior made him unpopular with a number of people, especially some influential older leaders. But the young Athenians richly enjoyed these conversations in the marketplace (called the *agora*), and thus Socrates acquired quite a following. Among his followers was the young Plato.

Socrates became a martyr. In 399 B.C., when Plato was about twenty-eight years old, the Athenian court sentenced Socrates to die. He was charged with corrupting the youth of Athens and with not believing in the traditional Greek gods. Apparently Socrates had angered too many prominent citizens and was, perhaps, influencing too many young men to question the political activities of the controlling powers.

Plato wrote many dialogues and in more than twenty of them Socrates is the main character. For example, in his dialogue the *Apology* Plato recounts the proceedings of Socrates' trial. In the *Crito* he dramatizes Socrates' reasons for not escaping from prison, when he had every opportunity. And in the *Phaedo* Plato presents, along with a discourse on death and immortality, a stirring account of Socrates' death by the poisonous hemlock. In Plato's most famous dialogue, *The Republic*, Socrates is portrayed in his middle years, perhaps fifteen or twenty years before his condemnation by the Athenian leaders.

Combined with the defeat of Athens and the reign of terror that existed in Athens for several years after the war, the circumstances of Socrates' death probably convinced Plato once and for all that governments are bad and will remain so until philosophers are kings. *The Republic* strongly argues that existing forms of government are neither appropriate for the human good, nor are they just. Plato asserts that philosophers must rule—only then will true justice prevail, only then will there be health in the souls of individuals and in the soul of the state.

After twenty-four centuries Plato continues to be one of the most celebrated, loved, and widely read philosophers in the Western world. Some scholars consider all philosophical writing since Plato's merely as footnotes to his thought. Ralph Waldo Emerson said, "Out of Plato come all things that are still written and debated among men of thought." Thus, to study Plato is to contemplate ideas that have fascinated, absorbed, and perplexed people for centuries; it is to have a grasp on wisdom.

# THE BOOK

## Some Basics About the Book

*The Republic* is not a novel; it has no plot. Yet it does share several elements with novels: it has characters, conflict, action, and themes.

Socrates is the main character and the narrator of the action. The action, however, is not action in the usual sense. There are no murders or car chases or torrid love scenes. The dynamic discussions of *ideas*, in the form of friendly but rigorous *arguments*, comprise the action. Thus, *The Republic* is intellectually exciting.

The principle of justice—the principle of the organization of the Good Life—is the central theme of *The Republic*. Other themes, however, are inextricably interwoven with the theme of justice. There is the theme of knowledge; the well-ordered life must be guided by wisdom. And wisdom, in turn, depends on a particular kind of education. Also, there are the themes of the place of poetry and art in a good society and of the philosopher's relationship to the political community. In sum, *The Republic* is an examination of the Good Life, that is, of the possibility of harmonizing the various excellences of human souls and societies into a visionary model of the Good Life for all.

*The Republic* is traditionally divided into ten books. Probably each book represents the amount of material that could be included on a papyrus roll. Hence, as you will discover, some strands of the discussion are interrupted by book divisions. The books do not designate separations of ideas but are simply the accidental beginnings and endings necessitated by ancient book production methods. Nevertheless, because most translations of *The Republic* follow the traditional divisions, this guide is organized that way.

Also, in the margins of most editions of *The Republic* you will notice numbers and letters. For example, Book I begins with the number 327, followed by "b," "c," and then the number 328. Book X ends at 621d. These numbers and letters have been the standard way of referring to passages in Plato's dialogues since the Stephanus edition of 1573. In this guide the Stephanus pagination will be used to refer you to the separate arguments within each book of *The Republic*. The occasional quotations in the guide are from Paul Shorey's English translation of *The Republic* (Loeb Classical Library, 1930).

# Socrates as a Character

To appreciate both the dialogue form and the substance of *The Republic*, it helps to have an understanding of the character Socrates. First of all, Socrates claims to have no knowledge. He is not a formal teacher who demands money for his marketplace wisdom, nor is he an introspective, solitary sage who sits above the world on a mountain of knowledge. Instead he is a gregarious man who enjoys the public examination of ideas; he is a philosopher, a seeker—not a knower—of truth. Throughout *The Republic* he warns his companions that his words should not be written in stone; that is, he's not dogmatic or tied to a system of doctrine. However, once the exploration of the meaning and significance of justice is initiated, he is willing to lead the inquiry and to pursue persistently the logical strands of the discussion.

In his dialogues Plato portrays Socrates as a social man, inquisitive and intense, witty and insightful, and with a kind of arrogance that goes with the territory of knowing one's own talents and limitations. But is Plato's portrayal of the character Socrates faithful to the historical Socrates?

Practically nothing is known for certain about the "real" Socrates. And scholars disagree on what sources present the truest account of the man. Some scholars say to turn to Xenophon, an Athenian writer younger than Plato who depicted Socrates as an excellent preacher of practical ethics, yet as a man uninspired by philosophic speculation and unconcerned with theoretical discussions. Other scholars say to go to the writings of Plato's student, Aristotle. And yet others declare that Socrates is a pure myth, a legendary figure who never actually existed. Nevertheless, more scholars than not believe that Plato's dialogues present the best account of the real Socrates. But, in fact, whether there was a real Socrates and what he was like remain a mystery.

The Republic does not offer you a complete picture of the character Socrates. To know more about him you would have to read a number of Plato's other dialogues. But it is not necessary to read these other dialogues to see the qualities that so greatly inspired Plato (whether an imaginative inspiration or a real-life one). Socrates' lucid, witty, exciting intelligence is apparent throughout The Republic.

Scholars disagree on the time of the setting of The Republic. Some say 421 B.C., others say 411 B.C., which places Socrates' age at either fifty or sixty years old. Perhaps Plato had no particular date in mind when he

wrote the dialogue a number of years after Socrates'
death (399 B.C.), except to set it during a pause in the
Peloponnesian War.

# Form and Style

Plato was not only a great philosopher, he was also
a dramatic artist. His exciting presentations of intense,
unique conversations offer you the opportunity to
participate in profound discussions and to see language beautifully used. Both his ideas and his artistry
have resisted time. His work is as relevant today as it
was twenty-four centuries ago. Why do Plato's writings continue to fascinate?

Plato had a knack for interweaving the elements of
high drama with complex philosophic thought. The
expressive form he used is called a *dialogue* (a word
that comes from the Greek language and means "conversation between two or more people," or, literally,
"talking through" some issue). Plato wrote more than
thirty dialogues and is often credited with having
invented the dialogue as a literary form. *The Republic* is
his most famous dialogue, perhaps the most provocative, and one of the longest.

But what exactly are Socratic dialogues? First, they
are conversations in which a man called Socrates is
almost always the main speaker. Generally the dialogues begin with Socrates casually meeting some
people in the street. After a few pleasantries are
exchanged Socrates turns the conversation into a philosophical discussion. And during the course of the
conversation, he finds that his companions are using
terms that are vague and ambiguous, that demand

clarification and definition. Thus, he asks them to explain their terms, such as "justice," "knowledge," or "love."

Through a series of questions, Socrates attempts to help his companions discover their own ignorance (the starting point of philosophy is the realization that you do not have knowledge) and then to lead them to greater understanding through the systematic search for knowledge. Plato calls this method of question and answer "dialectic"; that is, the process of playing one idea against another and of making analogies so that genuine insight may be gained. *The Republic* offers you many examples of dialectic.

Plato's dialogues are probably similar to confrontations Socrates actually had with Athenian citizens. Dialogues, then, are dramatic presentations of philosophical discussions. But beware! These conversations with Socrates do not always run smoothly. Arguments result; tempers flare. Yet Socrates inevitably emerges unscathed, victor of the debate. Even so, there are many moments of high drama in the dialogues. In some of the dialogues the humor is delicious; in others, there are declarations of outrageous devotion. Whatever the situation, Plato provides comic relief, reveals human frailties, and presents provocative discussions on principal concepts of human conduct.

Why did Plato cast his philosophical writings in the dialogue form rather than in the form of a scholarly essay? Some scholars claim that the young Plato, before he met Socrates, wanted to be a dramatic poet like Sophocles and Euripides and that perhaps he even wrote a few plays. Other scholars present evidence suggesting that Plato's works were performed in competitive, intellectual games during religious festivals. And still others believe that the young Plato, after watching and admiring the masterful debates of Socrates, wanted to re-create Socrates' teachings in a way that would capture the dramatic force of his mentor. Perhaps there is some truth in all of these views. After all, Plato was a superb dramatic artist who created thought-provoking, sometimes gamelike, discussions and debates similar to those Socrates engaged in with the people of Athens.

# The Dialogue

## BOOK I: WHAT ARE THE CURRENT VIEWS ON JUSTICE?

This introductory book raises the fundamental issue of the entire work: What is justice? Four views of justice are examined: 1. justice is speaking the truth and paying one's debts; 2. justice is helping one's friends and harming one's enemies; 3. justice is to the advantage of the stronger; and 4. injustice is more profitable than justice.

## Speaking the Truth and Paying One's Debts (327a–331d)

Many Athenians are celebrating the introduction of a new goddess in Piraeus, the port of Athens and the center of the democratic party. Socrates and Glaucon are returning from the festivities when Polemarchus sees them. He insists that they come to his home for some conversation with his friends. Socrates is persuaded. He cannot, it seems, resist this opportunity to discuss philosophy with a group of noble youth.

Polemarchus' father, Cephalus, is in the house. Socrates sees how old he has grown and wants to know whether old age is a difficult part of life. Cephalus says that he is glad to have escaped the "mad masters" of bodily pleasures and is now content. But he quickly adds that if he had not cultivated a good character he would be unable to enjoy old age. Then Socrates poses several rather crude questions: Do you think you endure old age easily because you are wealthy? Is acquiring wealth really the important thing in life? Socrates, who is penniless by choice, implies that men like Cephalus often forget about the conditions that make their kind of life possible.

Cephalus admits that his wealth makes it possible for him to live a well-balanced life. He does not have to deceive others, nor is he in debt to any god or any man. Socrates seizes on these remarks to talk about justice. He asks Cephalus if he means that justice—good conduct in relation to others—is simply telling the truth and honoring one's debts. This is precisely what Cephalus, the successful businessman, means. Because of his wealth he can die contented, his duties fulfilled. Thus, for Cephalus justice is a matter of self-interest, but also his view agrees with the laws of the city and with the traditional religious beliefs.

Socrates' objection to Cephalus is quite simple: Aren't there times when one should not tell the truth or repay debts? For example, if a man loaned you a gun, then became insanely jealous and asked you to return his gun so he could shoot his wife, should you return his weapon? Because Cephalus' definition of justice does not hold up in *all* cases, Socrates says that it is not a good definition.

Suddenly Cephalus decides that he must leave; there are yet more debts to be paid to the gods. He refuses to be drawn into a philosophical discussion, one that might threaten his cherished beliefs.

Cephalus' definition, like the ones of Polemarchus and Thrasymachus that follow, is found wanting. However, from each of the definitions presented in Book I something is learned that will be reflected in the principle of justice Socrates develops later.

## Helping Friends and Harming Enemies (331e–336a)

After Cephalus leaves, the discussion becomes more serious and more complex. Polemarchus carries on his father's argument. But unlike his father he is not concerned with the role of justice in religious matters. Instead, Polemarchus relies on authorities other than the gods or the laws. He borrows a maxim from the poet Simonides—justice is "giving every man his due." Socrates confesses that he doesn't know what the poet means, and asks, "What is it that is due, and to whom?" He knows, for instance, what the functions of such crafts as medicine and cooking are. But what is the function of the craft of justice, if indeed it is a craft? Polemarchus says that justice is benefiting one's friends and harming one's enemies. At last, Socrates has a clear statement that he can systematically examine.

Socrates' examination of Polemarchus' definition can be divided into three parts: 1. a look at how one can benefit friends (332d–334b); 2. an attempt to define "friend" (334c–335b); and 3. a criticism of the view that a just man can do harm (335c–336a).

1.  Socrates asks Polemarchus to explain in what ways justice can be helpful and harmful. Through a series of leading questions—Is the just man more useful than the farmer in producing crops? Than the builder in constructing houses? and so on—Socrates leads Polemarchus to the absurd conclusion that justice must be useless. And Socrates pursues this line of

reasoning to yet another absurdity. Because justice, according to Polemarchus' definition, appears to be the craft of keepers of things not in use (money and property), and because good keepers are in a position to be the best thieves, justice appears to be the craft of thieving, to the benefit, of course, of one's friends.

**2.** Polemarchus protests. Socrates concedes that maybe his problem is not knowing what Polemarchus means by "friend." Polemarchus responds that friends are those who we think are good and helpful to us. But, Socrates asks, can we be mistaken about who our friends, and enemies, are? If so, we may be helping or harming the wrong people, which could not be justice. A contradiction is reached: Justice can both help and harm friends. Polemarchus is forced to be more precise about what he means by "friend." He says "that the man who both seems and is good is the friend."

**3.** At this point, Socrates focuses on the crucial aspect of his quarrel with Polemarchus' definition. Surely it cannot be the function of justice to harm anyone at all. Don't we consider justice to be an excellence of character? And no excellence—whether that of horses or humans—is ever achieved through destructive means. The function of justice is to improve human nature. Whatever else it may be, justice is a form of goodness that, by its very nature, cannot participate in anything injurious to someone's character.

---

**NOTE:** The method of argumentation in this section is worth noting carefully. Socrates' discussion with Polemarchus is a superb example of what is sometimes called the *Socratic method*. Said to be invented by Socrates (and, obviously, named for him), the Socratic method is a philosophical technique for discovering knowledge through question and answer. Socrates, claiming to have no knowledge, encourages others to answer a general question. Here the question is "What is justice?" He then proceeds to show the inadequacies of each definition by producing counterexamples, that is, by producing examples that expose the biased nature or the narrow scope or the outright falsity of a definition. These exercises in thinking are not entirely negative. The ultimate goal is always to discover that which is true, good, universal.

---

## The Advantage of the Stronger (336b–347e)

Thrasymachus roars "like a wild beast" into the discussion. He angrily accuses Socrates and Polemarchus of talking rubbish—all this question and answer business! He wants to know why Socrates does not just say what he means. Thrasymachus, a sophist, likes to give long speeches without being interrupted by questions. Any other form of teaching, he believes, shows weakness.

This scene provides comic relief from the seriousness of the preceding discussion. Socrates describes himself as trembling and frightened by Thrasymachus' outburst. But you know better. Socrates is setting Thrasymachus up for the kill.

The long argument of this section can be divided into four parts: 1. an attempt to arrive at a precise definition of "ruler" (337d–341b); 2. a comparison between leadership and other crafts (341c–342e); 3. a speech by Thrasymachus on justice (343a–344c); and 4. a discussion on why rulers choose to rule (344d–347e).

**1.** Socrates begins his calm, methodical attack on the snarling Thrasymachus by luring the sophist into presenting his own view on justice. But first Thrasymachus wants to be paid for his information. The young men, not wanting to be denied a good fight, agree to put up the money.

Like Polemarchus before him, Thrasymachus thinks that the notion of justice can be summed up in a few words. He says "the just is nothing else but the advantage of the stronger." As is the philosopher's fashion, Socrates inquires into the meaning of Thrasymachus' definition. Thus begins a lively discussion, again exemplifying the Socratic method, on what is and is not to the advantage of the stronger.

Socrates and Thrasymachus agree that the "stronger" are those who rule and establish law, and that being just is advantageous. But they disagree on to whom being just is advantageous. Is it to the just man himself? Or is it to the ruler who determines what is and is not just?

Thrasymachus puts forth an extreme form of the doctrine "might is right." For him being just is obeying the laws of rulers. Further, he claims that rulers make laws for the purpose of increasing their own power and wealth. Just men, therefore, are weak and powerless in comparison to rulers. But Socrates soon has Thrasymachus agreeing that sometimes rulers make errors of judgment and that, in such circumstances, the rulers' advantage may be thwarted if their orders are obeyed. Thrasymachus finds that he must qualify his claim: Rulers who make mistakes are not rulers, in the precise sense of the term.

**2.** At this point Thrasymachus unwittingly lets into the argument a thoroughly Socratic notion: Rulers of any kind—of states, of arts, of crafts—must be guided by knowledge. Rulers can be considered rulers only when they are performing their proper function. But what is their function? Is it not similar to the function of other useful arts? Doctors serve the sick; ship captains serve sailors; horse trainers serve horses. Knowing how to serve well, Socrates implies, is the special knowledge of each profession. Rulers must know how to serve the interests of the entire state. Thus, like other professionals, rulers seek not their own advantage, but the advantage of those who need their help.

3. Flustered by the turn the discussion has taken, Thrasymachus insults Socrates (who, you can imagine, is smiling tolerantly, as one might smile at an angry, chastised child). Then he plunges into a speech, thinking, no doubt, that by drawing on his powers of persuasive rhetoric he can win the argument and the admiration of the attentive young men. After all, Socrates' preceding argument was not an especially good one. But Thrasymachus' rhetoric does not help his cause. He makes a rather tactless comparison between shepherds who fatten sheep for their own appetites and rulers who fatten people for the same reason. And he raises a controversial issue that will guide much of the discussion of *The Republic*—the greatest happiness belongs to the wrongdoers (tyrants, for example), not to those who are wronged.

4. Instead of immediately attacking this last statement, Socrates presents his belief that true rulers do not rule willingly. Again he compares the function of rulers to the functions of other professionals. He says that the aim of true rulers is to provide for the welfare of the state and that true rulers are more or less forced into leadership in order to avoid being ruled by people of less ability than themselves. Why should rulers want to rule? Is it not better to be provided for than to

provide for others? Because leadership is such a demanding, often thankless task, rulers, like other craftsmen, deserve financial rewards for their services.

---

**NOTE:**     In this section you should note the comparisons that Socrates introduces into the argument. He compares the usefulness of rulers to the usefulness of doctors, merchants, ship captains, and horse breeders. This technique is sometimes called "argument from analogy." Plato relies heavily on such arguments throughout *The Republic*.

In part, Plato employs analogy to make the point that statesmanship is like any other useful art or craft because it takes special skill and knowledge. But also Plato uses argument from analogy to persuade you to accept his views. Thus argument from analogy is a technique of persuasive rhetoric. With all forms of persuasive rhetoric ("propaganda" is the pejorative word), you should maintain a critical outlook. Comparisons of unlike things may be misleading, may be unfair and, more significantly, may cause you to accept as true a statement that is false. And yet arguments from analogy often clarify otherwise foggy concepts.

---

## Injustice Is More Profitable than Justice (347e–354c)

Now Socrates turns to the question of whether justice is good or bad. Logically speaking, Socrates has misplaced priorities: He is trying to determine the value of justice before he has defined justice. But he wants to maintain the interest of his audience. Young men, he knows, often grow weary of prolonged analytical discussions.

In the three stands of the following argument, Socrates attempts to refute Thrasymachus' claims that 1. being unjust is wise and good (348c–350c); 2. injustice is power (350d–352c); and 3. the unjust are happier than the just (352d–354c).

**1.**   Socrates wins the first point through a chain of complicated, if not incorrect, reasoning. Using argument from analogy, he compares the art of living well with the musician's art. The musician has knowledge of music and in this way is better than the unmusical person. The musician, however, does not want to be superior to or "get the better" of others who share his knowledge; rather, he wants only to be superior to the unmusical person. The same is true of the just man; he wants to outdo the unjust man but not those of his kind, the just. On the other hand, the unjust man wants to be superior both to those like and unlike himself. The unjust man is incredibly selfish and seeks only his own advantage. Socrates says that people who are good and wise do not want to be superior to or get the better of those who are like themselves. Thrasymachus agrees. Thus he is trapped into conceding that the unjust person cannot be good and wise. A strange argument, but a happy conclusion.

**2.**   With little difficulty, and certainly with reasoning more comprehensible than in the preceding argument, Socrates shows that injustice cannot be power because there is no loyalty among the unjust, no honor among thieves. Thrasymachus has to agree, based on his earlier statements, that unjust people are immensely selfish and so do not readily band together to achieve common goals. Continual dissension and hostility create chaos, not the powerful achievement gained by people working together harmoniously.

**3.** In the previous arguments Socrates demonstrated that justice is a virtue, a human excellence. He now has to show that human action in accordance with excellence brings happiness. Again Socrates uses analogies: The excellence of eyes is to see, of ears to hear. Excellence in these things, as in all others, means doing well in performing one's function. People who do well are blessed and happy. Thrasymachus agrees with Socrates' statements so far. Then Socrates reminds him that he had earlier conceded that justice is an excellence of character. Therefore, it must follow that the just person is the happy person.

Socrates concludes by summing up all three strands of the argument: Injustice is never more profitable than justice no matter how, dear Thrasymachus, you argue. Yet, although Thrasymachus has been soundly refuted, Socrates realizes that his argument is incomplete. The crucial issue—what is the nature of justice—has not been resolved. Justice is an excellence of human character and a source of happiness. But knowing these things is just a beginning. What is the just life? More investigation is needed. And so, on to Book II.

## BOOK II: JUSTICE WRIT LARGE

In Book I Socrates won one argument after another. Yet so far he has not seemed to provide any useful insights on how to live life well.

Glaucon and Adeimantus, ambitious young men with every prospect for successful political careers, are dissatisfied with his arguments. They agree with the spirit of his views—certainly justice must be more desirable than injustice. But they want to be entirely persuaded and they want some practical guidance. After all, Thrasymachus' teachings are attractive and seem more realistic than Socrates'. Why, in their pursuit for political glory, should they be hampered by considerations of fairness to others?

Such vital questions as how to live well and why people should conduct themselves with a watchful eye to the well-being of others are not simple to answer. Socrates perceives that a comprehensive account of the just life is needed. He pursues this task in the remaining books of *The Republic*, but not without some prodding from the young men.

Book II begins Socrates' description of the nature of justice and its place in the Good Life. This book can be divided into three sections: 1. Glaucon and Adeimantus' statement of the problem; 2. the origins and needs of the state; and 3. the excellence and education of the guardians.

## Statement of the Problem (357a–367e)

Glaucon, an able student of the Socratic method, questions the method's master. He agrees with Socrates that justice is a good thing, but what kind of a good thing is it? He offers Socrates three possibilities: Some things are done simply because they are good in themselves (for example, listening to music); other things are both good in themselves and have useful consequences (for example, eating); and yet other things are painful but have good consequences (for example, taking medicine). In which category do just things fall?

Socrates says that justice "belongs in the fairest class, that which a man who is to be happy must love both for its own sake and for the results."

But Glaucon sees no substance in this answer. For one thing, the *hoi polloi* (Greek for "the common people" or "the vulgar masses") think that being just is no more than a painful necessity for maintaining a good reputation and for succeeding in business or politics. Perhaps, Glaucon says, Thrasymachus has the best advice: Discard these pretensions of justice and go after what you want!

Glaucon confesses that he does not really believe Thrasymachus' philosophy, but neither does he see any good reasons for believing that the just life is better than the unjust. What he desires from Socrates is to hear how the life of justice is good in itself and by itself. In other words, Glaucon is saying: Socrates, give us your vision of perfect justice uncontaminated by other human excellences and uncontaminated by any good consequences other than justice itself.

---

**NOTE:**      This is an unusual request. Yet here Glaucon introduces the central theme of *The Republic*—"justice" as the principle of the organization of the various excellences of men and states and not as a reward for good deeds. You'll discover that this principle is dependent on knowledge. Thus the themes of justice and knowledge are interwoven in Plato's treatment of the Good Life. However, significant elements of life other than justice and knowledge are denied to the upper classes (warriors and rulers) of the just state—for example, love, art, privacy, freedom, private property. Therefore, when you read Socrates' description of the just state, consider the following questions: What is "ideal" about the just state? What would it be like to live in a totally efficient, perfectly organized state? Does Plato believe that his state is well rounded and ideal in all ways or is he carrying an

ideal of justice to its logical, though impractical, conclusion? What does Plato mean by "ideal"? What are
the advantages and disadvantages of the just state? Is
the perfectly just state also perfectly lopsided in what
it offers its citizens?

---

To illustrate his perplexities, Glaucon presents the
Myth of Gyges' Ring. Gyges, a shepherd, found a
ring that could make him invisible with only a twist of
the band. With such power the good shepherd soon
became corrupt. He first seduced the king's wife,
killed the king, and then took over the kingdom.

Using this myth as an example, Glaucon presents
you with a choice between two extremes: Would you
rather be a totally self-seeking, unjust person who
seems to others to be the fairest and kindest of people,
or the totally just soul whom others believe is the most
despicable of characters? In other words, what are the
advantages of being just if your good character and
good deeds are not recognized and praised? Is the
best life to seem just without being just?

Socrates starts to reply to Glaucon's questions, but
Adeimantus speaks first. Adeimantus feels that the
most essential question remains to be asked: What
does our educational system teach about the benefits
of good conduct toward others? Do our parents and
teachers recommend good conduct because of the
fine reputation and social prestige that it will bring us?
The well-schooled Adeimantus recites several passages from the poets Hesiod and Homer in support of
his case. These poets argue that even the gods can be
bribed. The wrongs hidden from people cannot be
hidden from the gods, but after sumptuous sacrifices
(such as the wealthy Cephalus is probably making in
his garden at the moment), the gods forgive and forget wrongs. Thus, neither laymen nor poets have ever

condemned injustice or recommended justice except
for the respectability and rewards that result from
each. Adeimantus concludes by admonishing Socrates:

> Do not, then, I repeat, merely prove to us in argu-
> ment the superiority of justice to injustice, but
> show us what it is that each inherently does to its
> possessor—whether he does or does not escape
> the eyes of gods and men—whereby the one is
> good and the other evil. (367e)

Although they enjoy an arousing philosophical
argument, Glaucon and Adeimantus are practical
young men who want realistic answers to important
questions on how to live. The brothers are questioning their upbringing and their education. The poets
and sophists say one thing; Socrates says another.
Whose lead should they follow?

## Origins and Needs of the State (367e–374d)

From here on, Socrates does most of the talking. He
praises Glaucon and Adeimantus for their fine elabo-
rations on Thrasymachus' arguments and then agrees
to defend justice, as best he can, against Thrasymachus' vicious attack.

Socrates begins with a warning: "The inquiry we
are undertaking is no easy one but calls for keen
vision." The inquiry is, in fact, no less of a task than
looking into the very nature of the soul, of human
character. As Socrates says, to see justice in the soul
takes keener vision than most people possess. Somehow justice must be enlarged. Socrates brings in his
conceptual microscope and enlarges justice in the soul
by describing justice in the state, in a community of
souls. After justice is visible in the state, it can be illu-
minated in the souls of individuals.

**NOTE:** Since the time of the Imperial Romans (Plato's first editors) readers of *The Republic* have often asked if this dialogue deals primarily with politics and the constitution of the state or with psychology and the moral character of the soul. The answer is that it deals with both. For the ancient Greeks no clear difference existed between politics (from *polis*, meaning "city" or "city-state") and psychology (from *psyche*, meaning "soul"). The Greeks viewed man as a social animal; for them the study of man is inextricably intertwined with the study of the community, of which man is a part. In other words, the psychological constitution of the individual and the political constitution of a state are mutually interdependent.

With Adeimantus' help Socrates constructs the first city. His construction is not an historical account of how societies originated; rather, it is an analysis of the parts of society that correspond to the basic needs of human life—at least, in the beginning. Socrates says: We will create a city, but its real creator will be our needs.

In this city people join together because no one alone can provide all of the necessities for civilized living—food, housing, clothing, shoes—and, at the same time produce quality items. The work is distributed so that "one man performs one task according to his nature, at the right moment, and at leisure from other occupations."

The city grows. Farmers cannot be expected to make their own plows, so blacksmiths come into being. Weavers cannot be expected to produce their own wool, so shepherds come to be. And so on. Before long the city needs items it cannot produce itself. Trade with other cities becomes necessary. Some people become sailors, others become merchants. And yet other people, those who are not intelligent but who are physically strong, become laborers, "wage earners."

In this city of bare necessities each profession possesses its own integrity. Yet Socrates wants to know where justice is to be found. Adeimantus suggests that justice resides in the harmonious cooperation of the different types of workers. Before this possibility can be explored, Glaucon interrupts. He accuses Socrates of having created a city of pigs.

Glaucon is not happy with Socrates' and Adeimantus' simple city. He protests that it lacks the luxuries of life—couches to recline on, incense to smell, gold and ivory to adorn the rooms, exotic food to eat. Does Glaucon introduce luxuries because he is fond of the prosperous, flourishing life of Athens? Or does he feel that Socrates has ignored the very real problem of human appetites and passions?

Socrates describes Glaucon's luxurious city as "inflamed," not healthy. If there has to be a city of luxury, then the simple city must grow in its appetites.

The irony is that the city Glaucon calls the city of pigs is not a "piggish" place. The appetites of the citizens are in harmony with the necessities of life and do not create demands for superfluous things that can result in greedy ambition and competition. The city of pigs is, in fact, the healthy city in which each person performs his task and, in return, receives what he needs.

Nevertheless, Socrates allows luxuries to be introduced into the city. He now adds riches and "culture"—poets and actors, chefs and beauticians. This inflamed city is, in effect, Athens. Like Athens, it must go to war to acquire new territory to satisfy the vast appetites of its people. War becomes a necessity. The city needs an army.

---

**NOTE:**    Once war is introduced, Socrates never again speaks of the healthy city. Why not? Perhaps the reason is that there can be no such thing as a healthy city. More likely it is because there is no lack of justice in the healthy city. The city of pigs was contented, harmonious, inherently just; the inflamed city—the city of warriors—is harsh, competitive, and in great need of justice.

---

## The Excellence and Education of Guardians (374e–383c)

The soldiers of the just city are called "guardians." Their appointed tasks are to make war and to guard the city from intruders. They are a special class of people. Like well-bred watchdogs, they must be savage to enemies and gentle to their own people. In other words, the guardians represent Polemarchus' version of justice; they benefit friends and harm enemies. But they must know to whom to be savage and to whom to be gentle. Thus, they must be able to make distinctions. To make distinctions well is to have a grasp on wisdom, and so the guardians must be endowed with a philosophical nature. To develop fully their innate abilities, they must receive an outstanding education—gymnastics for the body and music for the soul.

---

**NOTE:**    Under Socrates' plan, the state will control the education of the guardians. State-control of education was a new idea for Athenians. The Athenian family, not the city-state, provided for the education of youth, usually in private day schools. Here boys learned to read and write, to recite poetry and play the lyre, to do calculations and geometry, and to exercise. *Gymnastics* is the Greek word for physical training. The word *music* refers to all of the studies over which the Muses (nine sister goddesses) presided: the arts and sciences, including literature, history, philosophy, sculpture, song. Thus, when Socrates is talking about music he is usually referring to much more than harmonious, rhythmic sound.

---

In large part, Socrates adopts the Athenian educational curriculum for his guardians. Yet he deviates in a major way. He insists that most of the present literature used in schools must be censored. Here he is not concerned with the form of literature, but rather with the content. For example, he is greatly troubled by the poems of Hesiod and Homer that often portray gods and heroes as immoral, murderous, deceptive, vicious, unjust, feuding. To Socrates, these old poems—the staple of Athenian moral education in his time—contain many lies. Worse yet, they show gods and heroes doing things that most people would harshly condemn other people for doing. Children, therefore, should not be exposed to these "false stories." The Olympian gods, as presented by the poets, are not good guides for conduct.

In sum, Socrates argues here that young guardians should only study stories that present good examples of moral conduct. The aims of early education, he implies, are to mold minds and character.

In the next book, the discussion on poetry and on the education of guardians continues.

# BOOK III: THE BASIC EDUCATION OF THE GUARDIANS

In ancient Greece horrible forms of violence and deception filled the stories that young Athenians heard and recited. Blood and gore, death and destruction seem, in general, to fascinate people. But should young children whose characters are not yet formed be exposed to literature that presents violence as an expected and accepted part of human nature? To some extent, your answer reveals your views on the issue of censorship.

Book III continues Socrates' arguments for the censorship of children's literature. But before the end of the book Socrates leaves this topic and returns to his main consideration—a vision of the perfectly just state. Book III can be divided into four parts: 1. proper musical training; 2. physical training; 3. the selection of rulers; and 4. the Myth of the Metals.

## Proper Musical Training (386a–403c)

Previously Socrates spoke against presenting young guardians with gods who kill their parents, fight wars with each other, and assume disguises to deceive humans. We cannot allow children to hear myths that encourage improper conduct toward parents or treachery and deception toward friends, he said.

Now he speaks to the necessity of instilling courage in the young guardians. For this purpose, the stories of the poets are again harmful; they encourage the fear of death. Socrates recites a number of Homer's verses from *The Iliad* and *The Odyssey*. These passages describe the horrors of Hades (the Greek afterworld). Homer paints horrible pictures of life after death, where spirits are "wailing their doom," and "gibbering ghosts" are flitting about. Socrates suggests that such verses make the young believe that slavery, and almost everything else, is preferable to death. Thus, Socrates says that we must censor "the entire vocabulary of terror and fear" if we are to have courageous guardians.

What verses, then, are suitable for the youth to hear? Socrates answers—those which praise honesty, loyalty, self-control, moderation of desires, and disparage any form of self-indulgence. The poets must depict gods and heroes as models of good conduct.

The "topic of tales" is concluded. The next topic is that of "diction"; that is, the proper literary forms for the moral education of children.

Socrates categorizes literature into two forms: simple narration and imitation. He is not critical of simple narration, in which storytellers relate events as they heard or saw them. But he insists on purging the state of imitative literature in which storytellers pretend to be something that they are not. He believes that imitative writing—the theatrical works of tragedy and comedy in particular—must not be admitted into the just city. Poets must give up their imitative ways, their flights into fantasy, and stick to the facts. Socrates confesses to Adeimantus, who is a lover of the theater, that by rejecting the imitative arts, we lose enchanting entertainment. Nevertheless, tragedy and comedy must go.

---

**NOTE:**     If Socrates lived today he would no doubt be opposed to children viewing most television programs and movies, and to attending live theatrical performances. Also, he would probably forbid fairy tales and Mother Goose. What a void this lack of entertainment and fantasy would create in most lives!

Socrates is quite negative about any form of fiction. In fact, fiction to him is altogether taboo. And he makes no suggestions on what other forms of escape and entertainment would be appropriate. Why does he want to ban the theatrical arts from the schools of Athens? What negative effects can such arts have on the characters of the future guardians of the state?

---

The dramatic arts encourage people to identify with the emotions and experiences of villains and fools, so Socrates says. They show people expressing strong passions and as such cause the audience to experience laughter, tears, or fear. These are precisely the passions to which the guardians must not be susceptible.

Schoolboys in Athens not only read the poets, they also attempted to act out the scenes with vigor and expressiveness. They were, in Socrates' words, "to be good mimics." Socrates condemns the practice of asking boys to behave like conceited kings, kowtowed slaves, raving madmen, nagging women, or even blaring trumpets. If the young guardians are to imitate anything, it must be the pious, brave, sober men who they are to become. Mimicking the baser, lesser types of characters can "settle down into habits and second nature in the body, the speech, and the thought." Because most drama concerns troubled souls— unhappy, suffering, ludicrous men and women—it must not be allowed to influence the young.

Besides, in the just city each person performs only one function, and that function is performed for the good of all. The guardians' function is to be courageous, high-spirited, and loyal. Therefore, they must not imitate those types of characters unlike themselves.

Socrates' critique of poetry, then, is not limited to content; he also argues that the forms of poetry (including Homer's epics) are not suitable for moral education. What is needed is a form of literature that will extol the highest excellences of human nature. Could Plato be suggesting that philosophical dialogues—with such heroes as Socrates—are the most appropriate form of literature for young guardians?

In the just city, Adeimantus, an aficionado of the theater, must forgo the pleasures of the dramatic arts. And Glaucon, a musician, will be deprived of the pleasures of popular melodies. At first Glaucon is quite upset. But Socrates persuades him that, like speech, melodies can move the passions in primitive, uncivilized ways. Thus, musical instruments must be of the simplest sort (the lyre and the cithara, a stringed instrument something like a harp) and must imitate only "the rhythms of a life that is orderly and brave."

As you see, Socrates is a severe censor of popular forms of entertainment. He summarizes his reasons for dwelling so long on the need to purge the just state of certain art forms, by saying that "education in music is most sovereign, because more than anything else rhythm and harmony find their way to the inmost soul and take strongest hold on it." The just state and the just soul do not contain anything that is not beautiful—no tumultuous emotions and no raucous melodies.

## Physical Training (403c–412b)

Because guardians are the state's warriors and protectors, physical training (gymnastics) is an essential part of their education. Gymnastics, however, is not as important to Socrates as one might expect. Victory in battle most certainly requires physically strong soldiers who can endure continual stresses and strains. But Socrates believes that the secret to having a sound body is having a sound mind and a good soul. The soldier who is well trained in "music" will be physically healthy because he will not be ruled by unnecessary appetites and passions—gluttony, greed, lust, and the like—that lead to poor health.

---

**NOTE:** Plato's lack of emphasis on physical training and his concentration on moral training results from the need to educate guardians to oppose the appetitive part of the soul (represented, as you will shortly see, by the lower class, the producers). Guardians must be ruled by the rational part of the soul. The problem of overwhelming appetites was generated by the movement from the city of pigs to the inflamed city. In the city of pigs appetites did not need to be controlled; there was health and harmony in the soul and state. But in the inflamed city the appetites, if left unchecked, tend to rule and the only antidote is to educate people to have good characters—to be reasonable, courageous, and moderate. People with healthy souls take care of their bodies.

---

For Socrates, physical training complements musical training, but he sees no need to prescribe a program of physical fitness for the guardians. Instead, he says a few words against drunkenness and too many sweets. Then he launches into a long digression on the functions of doctors and judges in the just society.

The doctor's role in the guardians' education seems to be an appropriate topic for a discussion on physical fitness. But why does Socrates compare doctors to judges?

Socrates does not have many good things to say about doctors and judges. He views their presence in a city as shameful. Doctors and judges, he says, are needed for the same reason—to deal with problems generated by inflamed desires. People who disrupt the lives of others go before judges; people who disrupt their own bodies' balance go to doctors. People should arrange their lives so that medicine and courts are not needed.

To ensure such a healthy arrangement of the soul, guardians must be trained in and exposed to only the simplest (thus, pure) forms of gymnastics and music. In their early training, they are to know no evil in body or soul. Their education, therefore, is to be highly controlled and extremely rigid. But who will control the guardians?

## The Selection of Rulers (412b–414b)

The rulers of the city, Socrates says, will be chosen from the guardians. How will they be chosen?

Until the age of twenty (as you will see in Book VII), all guardians will receive the education Socrates has just described. Further, they will be observed from earliest childhood and, from time to time, given tests to determine their susceptibility to corruption and to measure their interest in the well being of the state. The best guardians—those who are intelligent, prudent in political matters, and morally excellent—will be trained to be rulers. They are the "true guardians"; the other guardians can be better described as "auxiliaries," helpers of the rulers. The ultimate ruler, then, will be an older, highly intelligent warrior whose primary characteristic is zealous, unflagging interest in promoting the good of the state. This ruler will be the statesman whom the lower order of guardians, the auxiliaries, will obey.

Socrates' just city is a "class society." He has now introduced all three classes of citizens: producers, warriors, and rulers. Producers (doctors, farmers, builders, and so on) provide for the citizens' physical needs; warriors protect the citizens; and rulers govern. Of the three groups, the ruling class is considered the most noble, and its members must be showered with great honors, in life and after, to ensure their continual love for the city.

## The Myth of the Metals (414c–417b)

Throughout *The Republic* one of Plato's primary goals is to unify social experience. He perceives a variety of conflicting elements in the constitutions of states and souls, elements that prevent harmonious functioning. Thus, he seeks to reorder experience in order to eliminate sources of conflict. A "class society" (which Plato's just state is) has an inherent source of discord: The largest class of the state—merchants, farmers, craftsmen, peasants, and others who form the state's economic foundation—may not accept rule by the elite order of the guardians. In turn, some of the guardians may resent the lack of personal freedom and lack of private wealth imposed by their position. The problem, then, is how to educate the members of each class to respect and to accept their stations in the life of the state.

To promote unity in the state Socrates proposes a myth, which he calls a "noble lie." This myth, the Myth of the Metals, will be propagated for two reasons: to illustrate that all people are brothers and sisters born of the same earth *(autochthons)*, and to impart a sacred authority to the unequal status of the three classes.

The myth goes like this: In reality, during all of the years of their education and training, the young Athenians are within the earth being molded with proper equipment for doing their life's work. When their education is finished the earth, mother of all of the citizens, delivers them to the land so that they can protect her.

Even though all citizens are brothers and sisters, the supreme deity fashions the young Athenians with three different materials, some more precious than others. The rulers have gold in their veins; the warriors have silver; the producers have iron or brass. Once the people are fashioned, they cannot change their basic characteristics, nor can they ignore their responsibilities to mother earth. Yet there may be, on occasion, golden children born to silver parents and brass children to golden parents. When this happens the children will be quickly appointed to the class in which, by nature, they belong.

---

**NOTE:**    One of the key issues of the Myth of the Metals is what is sometimes called the nature-nurture problem: Are people born with certain abilities and characteristics (nature/heredity), or do they acquire these through experience and training (nurture/environment)? In this myth Plato reveals that he believes men are *by nature* unequal. His educational plan (the nurturing process) functions to determine which children have the potential to guard and then to develop this existing potential. Plato believes that children of guardians will usually inherit the potentials of their parents. But he also knows that often the children of parents with good character and high intelligence lack their parents' qualities. On the other hand, children of ignoble parents sometimes exhibit superior abilities. Therefore, Plato makes provisions for social mobility based upon the demonstration of the children's inherent potential during their basic education, during the time when mother earth is nurturing each child in accordance with his nature.

What do you think about this myth? Has Socrates provided an acceptable rationale for having a "class society"? Will the people believe the myth? Glaucon thinks that the first generation of the just society will not accept it, but that their sons and grandsons will. Socrates remains skeptical on the myth's acceptance but hopes that it will help make the people "more inclined to care for the state and one another."

Socrates abruptly returns to the city's economic and educational composition. Besides having the proper education, he says that the guardians (both the auxiliaries and the rulers) must not possess any private property or personal wealth. Their food, clothing, and housing will be of the simplest kind—communal and provided by the state. Why? To prevent jealousy and corruption.

The guardians are public servants. In the private sector, however, the householders and other producers can own property and have money. The producers lack prestige; the guardians lack possessions. Thus, each class has its benefits and disadvantages.

In the next book, the discussion of the just city is continued.

## BOOK IV: JUSTICE DISCOVERED

Socrates has constructed an austere city with a rigid class structure and a disturbing lack of charm. Will people be happy living in this city?

Adeimantus, a member of the Athenian ruling class, seriously doubts that he can find happiness in the "perfect" city. He asks Socrates: Where is the happiness for the guardians? How can guardians be happy without such pleasures as owning fine houses and entertaining friends? In effect, Adeimantus is accusing Socrates of denying the rulers everything for which, it seems, they have established civil order—property, privacy, happiness.

Here Socrates attempts to justify the structure of his city, which, you will see, is also the structure of the good soul. This book has three major sections: 1. the happy state; 2. the virtues of the state; and 3. the virtues of the individual.

## The Happy State (419c–427c)

"Happiness" is an elusive term. What makes one person happy may not please another. Some people enjoy rock music; others prefer jazz. Some people like gourmet meals; others prefer meat and potatoes. And one of Socrates' criteria for choosing the rulers from the warrior class is the type of things in which the candidates take pleasure. In fact, Socrates said in the last book that certain tests would separate seekers of personal gain from seekers of the good of the entire state. The candidates who enjoy serving the good of the state will become rulers. "Enjoy," however, may be too strong a word. Socrates does not require future rulers to enjoy serving; he simply requires them to consider the state's welfare their top priority.

Adeimantus charges Socrates with not making the guardians happy. He echoes Thrasymachus' claim in Book I that rulers should have great personal wealth. There Socrates argued that the rulers' job is to benefit the citizens, not to increase their wealth. Here Socrates follows a similar line of attack, only now he has more ammunition—the structure of the city he has constructed.

Socrates begins his defense with a reminder to Adeimantus:

> . . . the object on which we fixed our eyes in the establishment of our state was not the exceptional happiness of any one class but the greatest possible happiness of the city as a whole. (420b)

In other words, Socrates is proposing a model of a happy state, not of a happy group within the state. And the happy state is one in which each class performs its tasks in accordance with its designated excellence—farmers to cultivate the soil, soldiers to protect the citizens, and so on. Anything that keeps individuals from doing their jobs well cannot be permitted in the just city. Contrary to Thrasymachus' view, rulers do not govern for their own happiness; their job is to see to the happiness of the city as a whole, to see that each class has a share of happiness that is appropriate to its function.

---

**NOTE:** You may now be wondering if perhaps Socrates has his priorities reversed. Can there be a happy state without happy citizens? In *The Republic* Plato is not actually concerned with the concept of happiness. (His student Aristotle, however, takes up the issue "what is happiness?" in one of the most celebrated books on moral philosophy, the *Nicomachean Ethics*.) The Greek word we translate as "happiness" is *eudaimonia*, which literally means "being well with the gods."

---

Adeimantus wants the just state to be a happy one. Like Thrasymachus he equates happiness with wealth. Thus, Socrates can conveniently leave the issue of the guardians' happiness and turn to the issue of wealth. He says that both wealth and poverty corrupt a city. One brings idleness; the other brings poor workmanship. Both bring innovation, that is, new ideas that distort the true aims of the state. The just state is neither rich nor poor.

Adeimantus, secret lover of luxury that he is, makes one last stand in defense of wealth. He asks Socrates: How will our state, possessing no wealth of its own, be able to wage war against wealthy states?

---

**NOTE:**     Now, centuries later, Adeimantus' objection to the wealthless state remains a concern to people who study or engage in foreign policy. What good is it to have a wonderful society if it has no means to rebuff the threats of other nations? Will that society—just or otherwise—be overtaken by wealthy foreigners if there are no goods with which to negotiate with nor any means for balancing power?

---

Socrates responds that the just city must not worry about foreign invasion. For one thing, it will be too poor to attract envy or interest; for another, its army will be notoriously tough; and, finally, it will use diplomats to convince other cities that their best interest resides in being allies with the just city, a city that wants none of the spoils of war.

You may not be convinced, but Adeimantus is. Now the conversation turns to tying up some loose ends: The population of the city must be regulated because it must not grow too large; wives and children of the guardians will be held in common because possessions of any kind must be discouraged; new forms of music will not be tolerated because "the modes of music are never disturbed without unsettling the most fundamental political and social conventions"; styles of dress and manner among the young must not be legislated but will, instead, be educationally ingrained; and petty legislation of all kinds will not be tolerated among the policymakers because it would not be fitting to dictate to "good and honorable men" what they can do in their daily activities. The good city, Socrates and Adeimantus agree, is established.

## Virtues of the State (427c–434d)

The perfect city has been constructed. Because it is perfect—"good in the full sense"—it has all four of the Athenian virtues: wisdom, courage, moderation, and justice. Now Socrates' task is to discover wherein lies justice. First he outlines a method of investigation. He will look at each virtue separately, determine where it resides in the city, and then see if any of the four virtues remains without a visible designation.

---

**NOTE:**    In Book II Socrates issued the warning that seeing justice in the soul takes keen vision. Now he hints that justice is not visible at all, that it is the virtue that has no physical representative. The vision he hopes to impart is intellectual insight, philosophical understanding of excellence in social organization and in the organization of the human *psyche* ("soul").

---

Looking for the virtues, Socrates investigates the city. First he finds wisdom. The city is well counseled, that is, it has good advisers who keep it running smoothly, efficiently, in perfect order. Who are these advisers? Not the carpenters who know about building, not the blacksmiths who know about metal, but the rulers who know about statesmanship. Wisdom has a home in the perfect state; it resides with the rulers. The rulers by their very nature and education are, while few in number, the holders of the special knowledge for leading the activities of the state.

Next Socrates finds courage. As he says, "there is no difficulty in seeing bravery itself and the part of the city in which it resides." Courage resides with the auxiliaries. From earliest childhood these soldiers have been trained in what to fear and what not to fear. Their training, Socrates says, has been like the process of dying wool purple, which takes careful preparation for making the dye hold fast. Unlike poorly dyed wool, the soldiers—the state's incarnation of courage—will never "present a ridiculous and washed-out appearance." Within the soldiers' unflagging adherence to the state's laws and protection lies the virtue of courage.

Then Socrates finds moderation (soberness and self-control). "Soberness," says Socrates, "is a kind of beautiful order and a continence of certain pleasures and appetites." In general, moderation is a kind of "self-mastery," a control of the worst part of the state by the better part. The better part is wisdom, the province of the rulers. Thus, moderation resides in the multitude of craftsmen and other members of the producing class. But moderation cannot be expected to reach these masses of its own accord. The masses must abide by the dictates of the ruling class, those who have wisdom. Further, Socrates says, moderation is not the sole province of a particular class of citizens. In the perfect state it must reside throughout every class.

Thus, wisdom, courage, and moderation reside in the members of the ruling, warrior, and producing classes, respectively, with moderation being a virtue that all classes must have. But where is justice? There seems to be no dwelling place for it.

Suddenly Socrates tells Glaucon that he has caught a glimpse of justice; that, in fact, "the thing apparently was tumbling about our feet from the start and yet we couldn't see it." Justice, he says, must be the principle of organization and harmony that guided the assignment of the other three virtues in the city. This principle requires that each person perform one primary social function in the city, a social service for which each person's character is best suited. Or, as Socrates says, justice is the "principle of doing one's own business."

On first view, this principle of justice does not seem to be very illuminating. Has all this time and effort attempting to understand the concept of justice been spent merely to conclude that the just city is no more than a city without busybodies and meddlers?

Socrates' principle of minding one's own business is more profound than it first appears. Upon reflection, you can see that Socrates has systematically constructed the principle of justice by using the other three virtues as building blocks, putting one upon the other. The producers must be moderate; auxiliaries must be moderate and courageous; and rulers must be moderate, courageous, and wise.

Socrates says that justice is a "residue" of the other three virtues. This means that the other virtues, when properly ordered and placed within the structure of a state, combine to create justice (perhaps in a fashion similar, to use a crude analogy, to the combination of fuel, heat, and oxygen that creates fire). Justice emerges from a well-ordered, smoothly running social organization. It is the fire of a properly ordered state. It is that quality which results when the individuals of the state perform their appointed tasks in accordance with their specific excellences of character. No class must meddle in the affairs of another class.

Farmers must not tell rulers how to make laws, and rulers must not tell farmers how to grow corn.

Thus, justice in the state is the proper functioning of each individual doing his or her own work for the benefit of all citizens. It comes about and is maintained through the dynamic interaction of the virtues of moderation, courage, and wisdom properly ordered. In addition, its presence in a state depends on the knowledge and wisdom of the state's rulers. Each class must possess the knowledge of what its proper function is, but the knowledge of the functioning of the state as a whole belongs to the rulers. Rulers, thus, are the guardians of what is good.

## The Virtues of the Individual (434d–445e)

Socrates returns to the question that began the discussion on the just state: What is justice in the individual? And he has meticulously worked toward a special formulation of this question: Is justice in the individual the same as justice in the state? In effect, Socrates has presented you with the opportunity to use your "keen vision" for determining the similarities between the organization of a state (political theory) and the "good" characteristics of individuals (ethical theory).

---

**NOTE:**    Before you begin comparing Socrates' ideas on the virtues of the state with those on the virtues of the individual, consider the substantial differences between politics and ethics. The words *politics* and *ethics* are derived from the Greek language. *Politics* comes from *polis*, which means "city" or "city-state"; *ethics* from *ethos*, which means "character" or "custom." In philosophy and humanities courses, a clear distinction is usually drawn between political theories (say, Machiavelli's *The Prince* and Hobbes'

*Leviathan*) and ethical theories (say, Aristotle's *Nicoma-chean Ethics* and Hume's *Enquiry into the Principles of Morals*). But for Socrates and Plato, the studies of politics and ethics concerned the same topic—the best way to live among others. Like other Athenian citizens, they would have had to stretch their imaginations far to think of human life without overtures of political melodies.

---

Not justice is "writ large." Socrates has explained that the harmonious functioning of a state depends upon each class of citizens performing its tasks and on not meddling in the affairs of the other classes. This specialization, he claims, benefits all citizens. But is the analogy between justice in the state and justice in the individual a reasonable comparison?

Here Socrates engages in some elementary psychology. His aim is to discover wherein lies the moral constitution of the individual. In the process of his investigation he arrives at the notion of a tripartite (three-part) soul: sensation, emotion, intelligence.

Socrates' argument for the existence of different elements in the soul is based, in part, on his observation that a person often reacts in opposite ways to the same situation. For example, a hungry man will normally eat a meal set before him unless he has good reasons for not doing so—perhaps health precautions against high-fat foods or fear of being poisoned. Thus, Socrates concludes, people do not act from one motivation alone. Like the state, an individual is a complex organism that can react to the same stimulation in a variety of ways. What are these ways?

First Socrates discusses the category of *desires* (appetite and sensation), thirst and hunger being "the most conspicuous members." He says that thirsty people naturally want to drink. But when they are ill and are informed that quenching their thirst could have dire consequences for their health, they abstain. *Reason*, in this case, masters desire.

There are, then, at least two elements of the soul—desire and reason. There is also a third—*emotion*, "the principle of high spirit." Like reason, emotion can master desire. Socrates presents a gory example of a man who wanted to see the bodies of those publicly executed, yet cringed at the thought of seeing them. He had two conflicting desires. Yet his anger, his emotion, mastered his desires. He ran to the corpses and cried out his anger over their crimes.

Although desire (sensation and appetite), emotion (spirit and will), and reason (intellect) are separate elements in the soul, often reason and emotion band together to win victories over the desires, which must always be controlled. This alliance in the individual soul is similar to the alliance in the state between the wise rulers and their high-spirited auxiliaries.

Further, as it must be in the state, the rational part of the soul, the wise part, must rule on behalf of the good of the entire individual. The high-spirited, emotional part must be made the subject to and the ally of reason. Together reason and emotion will preside over the appetites (the baser emotions and desires). In this fashion the entire soul and body will be strong, healthy, and beyond the corruption of the appetites.

It follows, then, that the individual is a miniature state. Justice in the soul is like justice in the state.

A diagram of the comparisons Socrates has made between the virtues in the state and in the individual may help.

| Virtue | State Function | Individual Function | Qualities |
|--------|----------------|---------------------|-----------|
| Wisdom | Rulers | Reason | Knowledge of the good for all |
| Courage | Auxiliaries | Emotions/ Spirit | Conviction on how to act |
| Moderation | Producers | Desires/ Sensation/ Appetite | Obedience to the wise and high-spirited |

Justice is the harmonious unity of all three elements under each of the four headings.

## BOOK V: WOMEN, WIVES, WARFARE, AND PHILOSOPHERS

With the analogy between the just city and the just soul drawn, Socrates is eager to move on to other topics. He introduces a new topic, four forms of injustice. However, before he can begin, his audience stops him. They feel that Socrates' discussion on justice is incomplete.

Polemarchus and Thrasymachus join the brothers Adeimantus and Glaucon in accusing Socrates of cheating them of an important part of his vision of the just state. In particular, they are intrigued by an earlier comment, which Socrates rushed by, that women and children will be the common possessions of friends. Socrates prefers to avoid this controversial issue. Most people, he claims, will find his ideas absurd.

Glaucon assures him that this audience will be polite. Yet the fear of appearing ridiculous or of generating hostility is not, Socrates says, why he is hesitant to speak. He explains that if he could speak with knowledge, he would be bold, but

> to speak when one doubts himself and is seeking while he talks, as I am doing, is a fearful and slippery venture. The fear is not of being laughed at, for that is childish, but, lest, missing the truth, I fall down and drag my friends with me in matters where it most imports not to stumble. (451a)

In this book Plato provides more details about the social institutions of the good state. You may find several of his ideas shocking, unacceptable, impossible to implement. Plato, no doubt, expected a hostile reaction, hence Socrates' demure attitude in the passage above. The Athenians were probably more appalled by these ideas than you will be. Nevertheless, the social reforms Plato suggests remain highly controversial today. In fact, you will see that except for the demand for philosopher kings, even Plato is uncertain of the feasibility of his suggested reforms. In several places he invites you to be critically alert. The social issues presented—sexual equality, marriage, and parenting—should stimulate you to question not only Plato's ideas but also your own beliefs on contemporary social institutions.

Book V seems to digress from the strand of arguments building toward Plato's vision of the place of wisdom and of the wise in the good society. Some scholars describe the first three sections of this book as an interlude, a time to digest what has gone before and to prepare for the abstract, metaphorical arguments that follow. However, a more accurate interpretation may be that here Plato is attempting to resolve problems that have the potential to cause conflict in the just state. Whatever Plato's intent, this book offers you the opportunity to think about the following five issues: 1. the equality of women; 2. the communal family; 3. the etiquette of war; 4. philosophers as kings; and 5. the Theory of Forms.

## The Equality of Women (451c–457c)

On one level this section is a serious attempt to provoke reform in the state by raising the status of women. Athenian women were a suppressed lot. They led lives of seclusion in the homes, were not given formal educations, and played no part in politics. On yet another level, these passages can be interpreted as a philosophic comedy. Socrates not only proposes that women should have the same educational and political opportunities as men, but says that men and women should share the same *palaistra* (gymnasium). To you this proposal may not seem at all preposterous, even if you know that all exercises in the *palaistra* were done in the nude. But to the Athenians it was a revolutionary and ridiculous notion.

Socrates argues for the equality of women. He advocates equal education and opportunity for both sexes. But he warns his audience, "we must not fear all the gibes with which the wits would greet so great a revolution." Even though Socrates acknowledges the inferiority of most women in terms of physical strength, he argues that sexual differences are not significant in terms of running a state. Intellectual ability and moral character are what count.

Socrates accuses Athens of being "unnatural" in its treatment of women. Women who have the "natural qualities" to be guardians must be educated in the same manner as their male counterparts. It is to the state's benefit to produce the best possible men *and* women.

At the end of this section, Socrates returns to the issue of naked exercising. Because the just state has thoroughly educated both sexes in good moral conduct, in the *palaistra* all people will be "clothed with virtue as a garment." And with this pronouncement, Socrates believes that the first "wave of paradox"—of encountering severe criticism and opposition to radical reform—has been surmounted.

## The Communal Family (457d–466c)

The second wave of paradox is that women and children will be held in common by the guardians. Socrates admits that this wave will be harder to surmount than the first. He thinks that he can convince his audience of its utility but doubts that he can defend its becoming an actual social institution.

As you already know, the guardians will eat, sleep, study, and exercise together. Hence, it is a small step to communal families. All property, including wives and children, must be held in common. But how can this policy be put into practice?

First Socrates says that the rulers (the highest order of guardians) must arrange all marriages. He compares the guardians to thoroughbred horses—"the best men will cohabit with the best women." There will be marriage festivals, but soldiers who excel in battle will be given "the opportunity of more frequent intercourse with women" because their offspring will be superior to the common lot. The offspring of the sacred couplings, those determined by the rulers, will be immediately taken to live with "certain nurses"; the offspring of inferior people, and all defective infants, the rulers "will dispose of in secret." And the rulers will engage in active population control; after all, the city must not exceed its means and bounds.

Socrates puts forth several other edicts: Childbearing will be forbidden to guardians outside prescribed age limits; nonstate-sanctioned sex will be taboo and offenders will be severely punished; incest must be avoided except on the rare occasions when the Delphic oracle approves of sexual intercourse between a brother and sister; according to birth dates following sexual unions, citizens will be told whom to call their sons and daughters and whom to call their brothers and sisters.

Will the rulers really be able to control the sexual liaisons of the guardians? Socrates hopes that a noble fiction, like the Myth of the Metals, will work. The guardians are to believe that chance (a lottery, perhaps?) determines their sexual partners, when, in fact, the rulers are busy manipulating with whom each person will cohabit, temporarily and for sex only. Increasingly, Socrates' just city becomes a place devoid of charm and pleasure. All romance is gone.

How does Socrates justify the abolition of the family and, in its wake, the abolition of romantic love? He says that it is for the good of the state. Romantic love (*eros*) distracts from this good, as do family ties. Why? Because loyalties become divided. Guardians must be trained to love the state first, foremost, and only. Brotherly love, love of the state, and love of wisdom are to be the guardians' loves because they bring the greatest possible unity to the state.

Socrates compares the state to a human body that has a wounded finger. All parts of the body share the pain of one part. Likewise, if one citizen suffers pain, the entire community shares it and must do something about it. Such notions as "my" pain and "your" pain must be abolished. Every citizen works together for the common good.

**NOTE:**    The complete abolition of the family, as you know it, is what Socrates proposes in this section. For Socrates to say that the second wave of paradox "provokes more distrust" than the first is a tremendous understatement. It is surprising that his audience does not protest loudly. But they do not. Why not? Do they think that Socrates is joking? Is he joking? Is he simply following the logical threads of his argument for the just state and in the process demonstrating the practical absurdities to which consistent argumentation can sometimes lead? Or did Socrates and Plato really believe that the good state would abolish the nuclear family in favor of a communal family? These are a few questions this section provokes.

## The Etiquette of War (466d–471e)

Socrates says that it remains to be determined whether it is possible for a communal family "to be brought about among men as it is in the other animals, and in what way it is possible." Glaucon is eager to discuss the possibility. But Socrates diverts his attention by raising the issue of how the just city will conduct itself in war.

As in their living conditions at home, so in war the guardians' lives will be communal. Men, women, and children will march to the same war drums. Children will go to war as apprentice soldiers. An additional advantage—and perhaps the most important one—to having children present at battle is that the guardians will fight better, both to protect their offspring and to impress them with their ability.

After discussing the role of children in battle, Socrates lists the state's responsibility to soldiers, and describes the ways in which guardians are to behave in battle. If captured, the soldiers will no longer be a concern to the state; if killed, they will be buried with great honor and their graves will be tended with extreme respect. In victory, the Athenian guardians will treat the defeated Greek nations with dignity and will extend their concern for all of humanity even to the defeated barbarian nations. No people will be enslaved, no booty will be taken, no women raped, no houses burned, no crops devastated. Socrates proposes such war conduct because he wants the just city to be a model for all cities, Greek and barbarian alike. The just city respects the dignity and the common humanity of all people.

## Philosophers As Kings (472a–476a)

The impatient Glaucon wants to proceed at once to the question of how the just state is possible. He has grown weary of philosophic speculation and wants to know if and how justice can be realized in an actual state.

Socrates reminds Glaucon that from the beginning the purpose of their investigation was to inquire into "the nature of ideal justice, . . . not to demonstrate the possibility of the realization of these ideals." To clarify his point Socrates draws a distinction between words and deeds. Words, he says, will usually be more precise than the deeds or objects that the words describe. In particular, he is referring to words that comprise a definition or a theory. No actual situation will conform exactly to a theoretical description. Take the geometrical idea of a *point*, for example. A point has no dimensions—no length, no width, no depth. Mathematicians, however, represent points with dots on paper or on a blackboard, and these dots have length, width, depth. These physical dots are merely representations of the idea of a point. A physical representation can only approximate an idea. Thus, the best anyone can expect in his attempt to represent justice in an observable way (empirically) is to arrive at an approximation of justice in the soul or state. Socrates says that all along the task has been "to create in words a pattern of a good state," that is, to produce an ideal model, a paradigm.

By distinguishing words and objects, speech and action, Socrates seems to intend, at least in part, to soften the disappointment that his audience may experience on learning that the good city can never be realized. Justice is an ideal, and cities, at best, are approximations of the ideal of justice. But, more significantly, here Socrates is preparing the way for a discussion that transcends the nature of any city, just or otherwise, a discussion on the distinction between the actual and the ideal.

With fear and trembling Socrates is finally ready to let the "great third wave" of paradox roll up against him. He states the paradox, in perhaps the most often quoted passage of *The Republic*, in this way:

> Unless, said I, either philosophers become kings in our states or those whom we now call kings and rulers take to the pursuit of philosophy seriously and adequately, and there is a conjunction of these two things, political power and philosophical intelligence . . . there can be no cessation of troubles, dear Glaucon, for our states nor, I fancy, for the human race either. (473d)

For Socrates, the philosopher king is a necessary condition for turning the poorly managed cities, as he believes all are, into approximations of the theoretical model of the ideal city.

Meanwhile, back in Cephalus' home, the idea that philosophers must rule shocks Glaucon. He warns Socrates that he should immediately defend his statement lest he be viciously attacked by the leading citizens (which, of course, he ultimately was).

Socrates is prepared to defend philosophy. He begins by defining *philosopher*. His definition rests on a comparison between true philosophers who are the best candidates for political leadership, and amateur or counterfeit philosophers who should leave philosophy alone and follow the leadership of true philosophers.

A philosopher, says Socrates, is a lover of wisdom. Like other kinds of lovers—of an attractive youth or of wine or of honor—lovers of wisdom desire not to possess merely a part of that which they love; they desire to possess the whole. Philosophers, then, desire *all* wisdom. (Socrates will soon explain what he means by this statement.)

Unlike true philosophers, amateurs are interested in only a small part of wisdom; mainly they are lovers of spectacles, that is, they are fascinated by particular sensations of color, shape, and sound. The spectacles of truth—of ideas, of all of knowledge—and not the spectacles of sensation, are the true philosophers' loves.

## The Theory of Forms (476b–480a)

What is the spectacle of truth that delights true philosophers and absorbs their attention? What is the whole of wisdom that they seek to know? These questions are difficult ones and not easily answered. In fact, Plato spends a considerable part of the remaining books presenting his theory of knowledge (*epistemology*). Embedded in his theory is one of his most famous doctrines, sometimes called the Theory of Forms. In the final section of this book Plato introduces the problem of knowledge. Here his treatment of the Forms is in no way complete and you may find it confusing. But in the coming images of the Analogy of the Sun, the Divided Line, and the Allegory of the Cave, Plato will present a much more thorough account of the whole of wisdom.

Now Socrates distinguishes *opinion* from *knowledge*. Those people—amateur philosophers, for instance—who believe in beautiful things but not in the idea of beauty itself, are living in a dream world of appearances and opinion, which is "the mistaking of resemblance for identity." On the other hand, those few people—true philosophers—who approach the idea of beauty and contemplate it in and by itself, apart from particular sensations, are very much awake because they are functioning in the mental state of knowledge.

Socrates then points out that *to know* is to know *some thing*; thus, knowledge must have objects. Likewise, *to believe* (to have opinions) is to believe *some thing*; therefore, belief also must have objects. What, then, is the difference between knowledge and belief?

Socrates argues that knowledge is infallible, that is to say that one cannot falsely know anything. To know some thing entails that the thing known exists, that it *is*. Further, he says that the objects of knowledge are unchanging and eternal. Belief, however, may be true or false. The objects of belief may or may not be real, may or may not exist.

---

**NOTE:**    Plato is making an important distinction between the faculties of the mind (such mental states as knowing and believing) and their domains as objects. Sometimes the mental faculties are described as the subjective realm of cognition, and the objects of cognition are described as the objective realm. In other words, the subjective realm is the internal ways in which people perceive some thing. The objects of the intellect—ideas—are external (objective) in the sense that these ideas exist apart from any one individual's cognition. The ideas exist no matter how you think about them. Indeed, the ideas exist even if you yourself aren't thinking about them at all. They can be grasped by people today as well as they were by the people of ancient Athens.

Also implied in this discussion is the distinction between the *actual* (the objects of opinion and sensation) and the *ideal* (the objects of knowledge and intellect). This distinction is crucial to Plato's Theory of Forms. There are *forms of things* (actual objects and experiences) and *forms of thought* (the way one thinks about the things of the world, the ideas one has about them). The philosopher seeks to understand the forms of thought—the idea of beauty, for example. However, to understand beauty in itself, one must see that the many actual instances of beauty all participate in the single idea of beauty. That is, beauty in itself is an idea (an intelligible form) that makes it possible to recognize beauty in the myriad things that come to be and pass away in the actual world. For instance, some things that are beautiful today (say, a vase of roses) may, over time, cease to be beautiful (shriveled, decaying roses). But the idea of beauty never decays, and always excludes its opposite, ugliness. Particular, beautiful things can *become* ugly, but the universal idea of beauty remains.

---

In this passage Socrates is telling Glaucon that true philosophers seek not the many spectacles of beauty, as do the amateurs. They pursue the *single* idea of beauty. The many examples of beauty belong in the realm of opinion and belief, of *becoming*. The Form of beauty, beauty in itself, belongs to knowledge and *being*. The objects of sensation—flowers, paintings, theatrical productions, and the like—come and go. The objects of knowledge—beauty, justice, velocity, and the like—are universal and permanent. If everything was constantly in a state of becoming, as the things of the world are, then there could be no knowledge. But true being exists in the form of the objects of thought which are, also, the objects of science and philosophy. Thus, knowledge of the Forms is the knowledge that true philosophers seek. In other words, one of the philosopher's tasks is to ask what can be truly known (not simply believed), and how it is that anyone comes to know anything.

Later, in Books VI, VII, and X, Plato will elaborate on and clarify the theory of knowledge that he introduces here.

## BOOK VI: THE PHILOSOPHER KING

Socrates begins this book by expressing his regret that the main topic of discussion—"discerning the differences between the just and the unjust life"—limits the depth of his remarks on the differences between the philosophic and nonphilosophic life. Nevertheless, the discussions here are devoted to explaining the nature of philosophers and philosophy. Five aspects of philospher kings and their special kind of knowledge are explored: 1. the attributes of true philosophers; 2. why philosophers are considered bad sorts; 3. the possibility of philosopher kings; 4. the Idea of the Good; and 5. the Divided Line.

## Attributes of True Philosophers (484a–487a)

Why should philosophers be kings? Answering this question, Socrates says, is the next logical step in theoretically establishing a regime for the good state.

Socrates has already defined philosophers as those people who are capable of understanding eternal and unchanging truths. This definition, however, suggests impractical theory-weavers who lack the interest and common sense to govern a state. The rulers' task is to guard the laws and pursuits of society. Are philosophers suited to such a task?

People whose task is to keep watch over things, Socrates argues, must have keen sight. Who has keener sight than those who have knowledge of the reality of things, of what things really are? Philosophers, by definition, have the keenest sight into reality.

Glaucon agrees, but says that rulers need other qualities in addition to intellectual vision. His remark prompts Socrates to list the characteristics of true philosophers.

True philosophers are educated from earliest childhood, as are all guardians, to act in accordance with the four excellences of human nature: wisdom, moderation, courage, and justice. But because they are endowed with an unusually fine native disposition (recall the Myth of the Metals where mother earth fashions rulers with veins of gold), their ways of displaying the four virtues are different in quality from the average guardian. Wisdom is revealed by their unflagging love of truth and by their continual demonstration of the spirit of truthfulness; moderation by their disregard of physical pleasures and by their immense delight in intellectual pleasures; courage by their understanding that death is inconsequential because they know that the essence of things, including human souls, is eternal; and justice by their lack of concern over petty matters, their integrity, and their understanding of the "wholeness in all things human and divine." Additionally, true philosophers are gentle, friendly, have good memories and, in general, are simply good people to be around and have around.

## Why Philosophers Are Considered Bad Sorts (487b–497a)

Adeimantus interrupts the discussion to accuse philosophers of misleading people who are inexperienced in "the game of question and answer." He voices the common man's suspicions of philosophers. Aren't philosophers more concerned with winning arguments than with reaching true conclusions? Don't they employ their superior powers of speech to distort the facts? Are the majority simply cranks and rascals?

Unlike what you may expect, Socrates agrees with Adeimantus' changes. Most people called philosophers are corrupt, he says, and those who aren't are, at present, useless to society. But there are good reasons for this deplorable situation. Socrates explains the reasons for the bad reputation of philosophers in two ways: 1. in the Parable of the Ship of State he shows why philosophers are considered useless (488a–489c); and 2. he discusses the ways in which potential philosophers become corrupted by the state (489d–497a).

1. The Parable of the Ship of State is the first of several images to come. Socrates uses images to help his audience understand complex ideas.

In this image the state is compared to a ship. The captain represents the people of the state. Like the multitude of people, the captain is big and strong but somewhat deaf, shortsighted, and with little knowledge of navigation, of how to govern a ship. The sailors, who represent the ambitious politicians of a democratic state, perpetually fight for control over the helm. Sometimes a sailor gains control by killing another sailor, sometimes by casting another into the sea. This struggle for power seems to be an end in itself.

Among the sailors there is a "true pilot" who understands the art of navigation and who should be the ruler of the ship. But the true pilot is not interested in the political quarrels, and so is ignored. He is considered an idle stargazer (after all, to navigate well a pilot must know the stars) and useless to the political intrigues of the sailors.

Socrates compares the true pilot to the philosopher. The philosopher is at present useless to society. But this fault, says Socrates, lies not with the philosopher; it lies with the public's attitude toward the role of philosophers and toward the democratic process.

Socrates says that the people should ask the man who knows how to govern to be the ruler. Doctors don't knock on people's doors to see if they are sick; the sick go to doctors for help. Likewise, philosophers can help the state to become healthy, but first the people must realize their need for knowledgeable rulers.

---

**NOTE:** The purpose of this parable is to create an image of a society (Athens) caught up in the game of political struggle. Such a society does not perceive its need for true guidance, and hence the philosophers helplessly watch the fray without being able to make any changes. Because of their wisdom and moral character, philosophers cannot enter the political arena, filled as it is with deceit, undignified begging for power, and instances of outrageous inhumanity. Because philosophers are not political contenders, and because they concentrate on universal truths rather than the popular issue of the moment, they are perceived by the public as useless.

---

**2.** "True pilots" of the state are few in number. But the state is not without many gifted young men who are potential philosophers. Why do the majority become corrupted and turn away from philosophy?

One reason, according to Socrates, is that the virtues themselves often corrupt the young. Adeimantus wants an explanation for this paradoxical answer. How can such good things as bravery and sobriety be the cause of bad things?

Socrates compares gifted young men to healthy seeds that are deprived of the proper climate and nutrition for growth. The best natures, he says, fare worse under poor environmental conditions than do inferior natures. The greater an individual's talents, the more susceptible he is to the influences of a bad education. Great crimes are committed by great minds.

Again, the fault lies not with philosophy. Socrates says that it lies within the values of an unjust society. In the public gathering places young people learn about the things of which their city approves and disapproves. And, naturally, they aspire to attain the honors bestowed on those who please the public. They adopt the values and practices of the city in order to acquire wealth and power. In the process they are diverted from seeking knowledge and are seduced into attending to appearances and opinion.

The perpetuation of false values, Socrates argues, is pervasive throughout society. No one group can be singled out for censure. The sophists merely teach young men the ways of succeeding in society—how to cater to public desires and how to flatter the collective ego. The poets and dramatists also seek public approval. Unfortunately, what the public wants and what it needs are two different things. The people are charmed by the appearances of beauty and have no interest in understanding beauty itself. Socrates concludes, "Philosophy, then, the love of wisdom, is impossible for the multitude."

Arrogance is another corrupting factor. The public adores handsome, intelligent young men. And it has great expectations for their eventual political success. This adoration, coupled with the pride of being well born in a great city, fills the souls of young men with "unbounded ambitious hopes" and causes them to be "haughty of mien and stuffed with empty pride and void of sense."

After being exposed to a wealth of corrupting influences, can gifted young men continue to love wisdom, to philosophize? They may pretend to seek knowledge, but in fact, Socrates says, they are, in a most cunning fashion, passing off opinion as truth and thereby bringing the greatest harm to society. The keenest minds are most susceptible to greatest corruption.

Can anyone be saved from society's corrupting influence? Can true philosophers emerge? Socrates uses himself as a case in point. He (and a few other good men) have been blessed with an incorruptible nature and with insight into the madness of the masses. The value of this blessing, however, is mixed: In the present society (Athens), the true philosopher is like "a man who has fallen among wild beasts." He is not only unable to benefit society, he is also likely to meet an untimely end at the hands of the savage horde. The best the philosopher can do is to withdraw from the political arena, keep quiet, and attempt to save his own soul.

## The Possibility of Philosopher Kings (497a–502c)

In this section Plato returns to the third wave of paradox: only a philosopher king can save the state from itself and from the corrupters it has engendered. It will take only one true philosopher to turn the state toward wisdom. (Could Plato be referring to himself?)

Socrates tells Adeimantus that a backward educational system is one reason why the present Athenian government is headed down the path of destruction. Athenian youth, he says, are introduced to philosophy at a time when they have neither the intellectual maturity nor the life experiences to make use of it. As a result, when they are older they think they know all there is to know about philosophy and so never again approach the discipline. This curriculum is the opposite of how schooling should proceed. The education of the young, Socrates says, should focus on physical training. Then, once the body is ready to support rigorous, intellectual efforts, the young should gradually be introduced to philosophy. Further, the end of life—once people are past the age of military and political service—should be wholly spent in philosophical pursuits.

Adeimantus suggests that Thrasymachus and Socrates' other hearers must certainly be opposed to this plan. Socrates chastises Adeimantus for trying to start a quarrel between him and Thrasymachus just when they are becoming friends.

**NOTE:**      Here Plato suddenly reminds you that Thrasymachus is still sitting in the audience. He wants you to reconsider the role Thrasymachus played in Book I. There Thrasymachus was portrayed as a "wild beast" disrupting a philosophical discussion; he was quite antagonistic toward philosophy. Now you can see that Plato was using him to represent the savage nature of the masses toward philosophy. But the once snarling Thrasymachus has been tamed. Thus, there is hope for philosophy being accepted by society.

Why has Thrasymachus become a friend of Socrates and a friend of philosophy? Perhaps he realizes that rhetoric (his particular strength and love) and philosophy can exist together. Perhaps he sees that philosophy is a gentle art not aimed at amassing great power and wealth but, rather, aimed at obtaining the best possible life for the people of the city.

Socrates says that bringing the city and philosophy together is by no means easy. But if Thrasymachus' anger toward philosophy can be assuaged, then, so can the anger of the masses. The masses can be educated to see that the philosopher's knowledge can bring harmony to the state and to their individual lives.

Although Socrates offers hope for the existence of a good state with philosopher kings, he includes conditions so difficult to obtain that the possibility remains highly unlikely. The philosopher kings will have to wipe the slate clean, that is, completely erase the present characters of men. The philosopher kings will be political artists who erase one portion of the picture of the state and paint in another until all of the parts resemble the heavenly model of the principle of justice.

## The Idea of the Good (502d–509c)

Socrates returns to the education of the philosopher kings. In Books II and III he outlined the basic education for all future guardians. In the remainder of this book and in Book VII he outlines the program of higher education for future kings. And he reveals what type of wisdom true rulers must have and love.

Adeimantus ventures to speculate that the philosophers' knowledge is gained from studying the principles of justice and the other virtues. To his surprise, Socrates disagrees. The greatest study is the *idea of the good*. Without an understanding of what is good, other subjects are worthless. Under the idea of the good all other ideas, including justice, are subsumed. What does this mean? Socrates is elaborating on the Greek notion that the greatest knowledge must be the knowledge of the ultimate values toward which all human life aims. The highest good for mankind is the most important object of knowledge and the source of all knowledge. Truth, beauty, and justice, for example, are only several of the ideas that comprise the most comprehensive study of all—the idea of the good, the highest form in the Theory of Forms.

Socrates says that most people believe that pleasure is the greatest good. But are not some pleasures bad? The good cannot be pleasure because to say that a thing is both good and bad is contradictory. The "finer spirits," on the other hand, claim that knowledge is the good. But this definition is circular because, when pressed to explain, the same people say that the good is knowledge and so no insight is gained. Could the good be a grand combination of pleasure and knowledge? At the moment, Socrates finds it easier to state what the good is not than to discover what it is.

Socrates admits that he has no adequate knowledge of the good. Glaucon nevertheless insists that Socrates attempt an account of it. Socrates offers a compromise: He will present an account of "the offspring of the good," the sun.

The Analogy of the Sun is Socrates' image for explaining the highest form of knowledge. He introduces his image by referring to *particulars* and *universals*. Particulars are the many things that can be seen with the eye, but not thought; universals can be thought but not seen. For instance, you can see a beautiful sunset—it is a particular—but you can understand beauty—a universal quality of sunsets and countless other particulars—only with the mind.

Light is what makes things visible and the best source of light is the sun. The sun is not identical with visible things, but it is the cause of vision itself. Likewise, the good is not identical to the objects of knowledge, but it is the source of knowledge. To see requires sun, to know requires reason. Thus, the idea of good is to reasoning as the sun is to seeing. As Socrates says, the idea of the good gives "truth to the objects of knowledge and the power of knowing to the knower."

Just as the sun provides the source of growth and nurture to living things, so the idea of the good provides the very existence and essence of the objects of knowledge. Nevertheless, the idea of the good is not identical to the essence it imparts; it "transcends essence in dignity and surpassing power."

Glaucon complains that Socrates is overstating his case. What he means is that he doesn't understand what Socrates is talking about. The idea of the good is an elusive notion, as Socrates earlier warned. But, in yet another image, Socrates will attempt to explain the idea of the good, the highest form of knowledge.

## The Divided Line (509d–511c)

Using the Analogy of the Sun Socrates demonstrated that there are two ways of knowing the world (two types of mental faculties)—perceiving with the senses and comprehending with the intellect. He also showed that two kinds of objects (two types of reality) correspond to these mental faculties—visible objects and intelligible objects. Now Socrates endeavors to reveal the inextricable relationship between mental processes and objects of reality. In the image of the Divided Line he presents an outline of his epistemology (theory of knowledge). And at the same time this outline is a concise educational model of the kinds of higher intellectual training needed for detaching the mind from a preoccupation with sensation and appetite, and moving the mind toward an understanding of the principle of knowledge itself.

Although a representation of the Divided Line is provided below, before you look at it see if you can follow Socrates' suggestions in the text.

Socrates gives the following directions: Draw a line divided into two unequal segments, the shorter segment representing the sensible world, the longer one representing the intelligible world. (The latter segment is longer because the intelligible world has a higher degree of reality and truth.) Next divide each major segment into two subsegments that have the same ratio as the sensible to the intelligible. Label the entire lower segment "sensible world" and the entire upper segment "intelligible world." Within the sensible world fill in one side of the line with the labels "shadows and reflections" on the bottom level, and "physical objects" on the next level. As you see, shadows and reflections are merely copies or imitations of such physical objects as animals, trees, and the like.

Moving up to the intelligible world, label the subsegment above "physical objects" with the words "mathematics and hypotheses," and think for a moment on the ways in which mathematics and other sciences use physical objects in order to illustrate the hypotheses generated by the mind. Finally, label the top subsegment "first principles and forms." Although these highest objects of knowledge use the hypotheses below to foster an understanding of the nature of absolute ideas, they are not affected by the imprecision and distortion of the sensible world.

Having completed the hierarchy representing the objects of knowledge, fill in the other side of the line with the ways of knowing each type of object. Beginning with the bottom subsegment, go up the hierarchy labeling the subsegments as follows: "imagination and conjecture," "belief and faith," "understanding," and "pure reason and dialectic." Your diagram should look similar to the one below:

| Objects of Knowledge | | | Ways of Knowing | |
|---|---|---|---|---|
| Intelligible World | Forms First Principles | 4 | Pure Reason Dialectic | Knowledge |
| | Mathematics Hypotheses | 3 | Understanding | |
| Sensible World | Physical Objects | 2 | Belief Faith | Opinion |
| | Reflections Shadows | 1 | Imagination Conjecture | |

In Book VII Plato represents his theory of knowledge and his program of intellectual progress in a more vivid way.

# BOOK VII: THE HIGHER EDUCATION OF THE GUARDIANS

The depths of corruption and the heights of divine wisdom were the topics of Book VI. You saw how a society can unwittingly lead a gifted youth astray, and then what steps the soul must take to progress from the lowest level of awareness (the shadows of reality) to the highest level (the idea of the good). These topics may at first seem unconnected. Why does Plato discuss the corruption of youth by a corrupt society alongside a discussion of the most magnificent knowledge of rational beings? The Allegory of the Cave, which begins this book, brings these topics together in a provocative way.

Book VII is perhaps the most tightly written book in *The Republic*. All of its parts are tied to an explanation of the necessary educational experiences of philosopher kings. There are three principal parts: 1. the Allegory of the Cave; 2. higher education; and 3. the six educational stages of philosopher kings.

## The Allegory of the Cave (514a–521b)

An allegory is a tale that uses symbolic characters and objects. The Allegory of the Cave metaphorically presents a person's travels from ignorance to wisdom, and also reveals the philosopher's obligation to society.

This famous story is Plato's most vivid and sublime image. Some scholars suggest that Plato probably took the idea for the cave image from the mystery cults. It is said that one of the rituals of the mysteries was to put candidates for initiation into caves representing the underworld, and then in glorious light reveal sacred objects to them.

---

**NOTE:**     The image of the Divided Line in the previous book serves as an itinerary for the journey out of the cave. Your best method for understanding the cave is to refer constantly to the divided line as Plato guides you through the four steps from darkness into light. Also, several other considerations should occupy your mind as you read the allegory: In what ways does the cave represent a system of education? Why is it so difficult to liberate people from the bondage of ignorance? As an educated person, what are your responsibilities to your fellow man, to society?

---

Socrates begins the story like this: Imagine prisoners living in a cave. Since childhood they have been chained facing the rear wall of the cave, unable to move their legs or to turn their heads. Now imagine that some distance behind them and on a higher level of the cave floor a fire blazes. Between the fire and the prisoners is a low wall behind which people hold up puppets representing animals, human beings, and other objects. These puppeteers speak, seeming to give the puppets voices. The fire casts the puppets' shadows on the rear wall. These shadow puppets are the only reality the prisoners have ever known.

One day one of the prisoners is freed from his bonds and forced to turn toward the fire. The sudden burst of light is painful and he cannot see the puppets clearly. At the same time the prisoner is told that what he believed was reality is in fact an illusion. Because of his ingrained belief in the reality of the shadows (and because he can't see the puppets) he refuses to believe that his life has been spent looking at shadows of imitation objects.

Behind the fire there is a long, narrow path that goes to the cave's entrance. The prisoner wants to return to his chains, but he is dragged outside into the sunlight. This light is even more painful than the fire-light. He desperately tries to flee, but he is again forced to stay in the light. First he is able to see shadows of trees, people, and other things, then reflections in water. Eventually he looks at the things of the world themselves and goes on to contemplate the heavenly objects—stars, the moon, and, finally, the sun.

The final step in the prisoner's journey is his realization that the sun is in some way the cause of all things being visible. At this point the prisoner has ended his educational journey. He has climbed the four levels of awareness—from shadows, to sensible objects, to science, and, at last, to knowledge of the principle of all things—the idea of the good. He has been liberated from ignorance. His education is complete.

What began as a contented, painless, yet shadowy existence grows—and the growth is painful—into a marvelous realization of the source of all things, of happiness, justice, truth, beauty, and goodness. The world of imagination, the first level of the divided line, is not, it turns out, the beginning of knowledge. It is no more than a realm of comfortable delusions. It is the city where people constantly argue over things of no eternal importance (over shadows of the imitations of reality). The educational journey, the road to knowledge, begins when shadows are recognized as shadows, and such recognition is painful. It always hurts to realize that one's past beliefs are mistaken. But without this pain knowledge can never be attained. Knowledge begins on the second level of the divided line, with the realization that one's former beliefs were merely reflections of actual things.

---

**NOTE:**     But who, really, considers shadows to be real things? For Socrates the shadows are the opinions of society through which people filter their ideas about life. Most people, he implies, do not even see everyday events in themselves; rather, people see events through the dark glasses of social customs and values. Consider the issue of public nakedness in Book V, or the issue of censorship in Books II and III. Your opinion on such issues is strongly influenced by your upbringing and by your needs for social approval.

---

Meanwhile, in the sunlight, the liberated prisoner counts himself as truly happy. He delights in the beauty of truth and the wisdom of eternity. His happiness is disturbed only by an occasional thought about the poor, pitiful souls back in the cave. On the one hand, he wants to help his former companions, but on the other, he fears if he returned to the darkness his companions would greet him with hostility and ridicule. He would no longer be able to see their "realities"—and of course they wouldn't be able to "see" his realities either—and so they could not converse with one another. He would be taken for a fool or, worse yet, for an enemy of the people. Would he not be as useless to them as philosophers are in ancient Athens? Would he not be in danger of being forced into courtrooms to explain himself before the shadows of justice that keep the prisoners (the people of the city in the cave) from understanding men who have seen justice itself?

The paradox is that only people who have caught sight of the idea of the good—the philosophers—can act wisely in a city. And only they can educate others, can bring their chained friends out of darkness into light, from ignorance to wisdom. They have the "art of producing vision." Therefore, Socrates' task is to show Glaucon how the philosopher, the liberated prisoner, can be persuaded to go back down into the cave.

Socrates does not question that the philosopher must leave his supreme existence in the sun and return to the people. He says that

> the law is not concerned with the special happiness of any class in the state, but is trying to produce this condition in the city as a whole, harmonizing and adapting the citizens to one another by persuasion and compulsion, and requiring them to impart to one another any benefit which they are severally able to bestow upon the community. (519e)

The benefit philosophers bestow is knowledge of what is good for the whole. Besides, they owe it to society. They must pay for the education they have received, by serving the people of the state. So Socrates says to the philosophers: "Down you must go then, each in his turn, to the habituation of the others and accustom yourselves to the observation of the obscure things there."

The philosophers' reward for their services is that during their tenure as rulers and educators they will still be able to spend much of their time in intellectual pursuits (their special pleasure). Philosophers, nevertheless, must be forced to rule the state. Because they are not "lovers of rule," they will not want to rule—but they must. It's their duty, their function in the state. Only philosophers, Socrates says, know how to turn the souls of the people toward the idea of the good.

A circle has been completed. The philosophers were initially dragged past the shadow puppets into the sunlight. Now they must be compelled to go back into the cave to persuade the people there to accept their wisdom. The philosophers' educational process was long and painful, yet worth the effort. They have been liberated from the chains of ignorance. And they are happy in their wisdom. But the former prisoners must become liberators. They must educate their chained fellow men. How?

## Higher Education (521c–531c)

For Plato educational experiences must be connected in a sequence moving from the concrete to the abstract, from the objects of sense to highest principles and generalizations. The basic education of the young guardians, as you saw in Book III, is music and gymnastics. When the guardians get to be twenty years old, however, their education must be aimed toward drawing their souls "away from the world of becoming to the world of being." In other words, knowledge of the objects of the world, which are merely a continual stream of the generation and the passing away of appearances, must grow into knowledge of the eternal, unchanging forms. The guardians must learn to think abstractly. What kinds of studies have the power to teach people to think abstractly, to think well? Socrates believes that studies in mathematics and philosophy are the catalysts for intellectual growth. Thus, his educational program for future philosopher kings includes ten years of mathematics followed by five years of philosophy.

Socrates proposes five sequential courses in mathematics in which each preceding course is a reflection of the successive one—a solid foundation in arithmetic is necessary for an understanding of geometry, and so on.

First, the guardians will pursue *arithmetic*, the study of abstract numbers, because it awakens thought. *Plane geometry*, the study of eternally existing axioms and self-evident truths, will be their second course because it leads the soul closer to an understanding of the idea of the good. Third, they will explore *solid geometry*, the study of the third dimension, because it is a necessary prerequisite for understanding physics and astronomy. Next, *astronomy*, the study of solids in motion which includes the study of physics, will be investigated because the heavenly bodies exhibit such mathematical notions as speed, mass, and energy. And finally, *harmonics*, the study of musical harmony, will be pursued for an understanding of the mathematical relations found in beautiful sounds. (This latter study was advanced by the Pythagoreans, a mystery cult that greatly influenced Plato's thought and the group that first investigated the connection between music and mathematics.)

After ten years of mathematics, the scholars and future kings will immerse themselves in *dialectic*, the one true science, the search for wisdom—philosophy. Socrates says that all of the years of mathematical studies were merely preparation for this, the greatest of all intellectual pursuits. Socrates defines dialectic as the "inquiry that attempts systematically and in all cases to determine what each thing really is." It is the art that enables people "to ask and answer questions in the most scientific manner." In other words, it is Socrates' particular art. As you see in *The Republic*, one of Socrates' principal goals is to exhibit the art of creating conceptual harmony by unifying ideas that seem to conflict. Dialectic is the pursuit of an ordered, harmonious intelligence.

While discussing the guardians' course of study, Socrates connects higher education to the image of the Divided Line. The five mathematical disciplines belong to the third level—understanding; and dialectic belongs to the fourth—reason itself. Also, throughout this discussion, Socrates refers to the Allegory of the Cave, to the need to bring people out of darkness into light, which is the primary goal of higher education.

## Six Educational Stages (535a–541b)

The guardians' course of study has been outlined. The greatest study has been explained. What remains to be established are the ages and stages for pursuing educational aims. Here Socrates traces the six educational hurdles of the future kings.

Until children are seventeen or eighteen years old they will undergo a program of physical and musical training, the arts and sciences. They will not be compelled to study, but will be encouraged to explore their studies in a playful way. And by observing their play the guardian selection committee will be able to determine the natural capacities of each child.

Between the ages of seventeen and twenty, the most gifted children will engage only in physical and military training. These years will be so physically strenuous that they will have no leisure time for study.

Another selection of future guardians will be made during their twentieth year. These chosen will study advanced mathematics for the next ten years. And although they will not be introduced to dialectic, they will be tested to determine who are the most able to see the connections among the five courses of mathematics.

In their thirtieth year those passing the tests will study dialectic for five years. The teachers of dialectic will have to be exceedingly adept at introducing students to philosophy. They must not proceed too quickly (remember the blinding light of the sun in the Allegory of the Cave). The danger is that youth too often use dialectic as a sport rather than as a tool for discerning truth. The chosen class of thirty-year-olds will have orderly and stable natures and the desire to devote themselves "to the continuous and strenuous study of dialectic undisturbed by anything else."

Between the ages of thirty-five and fifty the future philosopher kings must spend their time in the darkness of the cave. Here they will engage in the practical affairs of the city, and hold commands in war. This exposure to city life will not only provide them with practical experience (and the opportunity to adjust to the darkness), it will also serve as a test of their ability to abstain from the temptations of wealth and from other appetitive corruptions.

Finally, at the age of fifty, those who have passed all of the tests will be selected as philosopher kings. For the remainder of their lives they will take turns ruling the city and studying philosophy. In death they will be honored. And here Socrates again mentions that women of ability will be among the philosopher kings.

Through this program of education and selection justice will become possible in the city. But what happens to the candidates who flunk the tests at various stages? And who will the teachers be? Socrates never answers these questions.

This book ends with a much too handy solution to the problem of the realization of the just society—banish all adults and begin the city with only impressionable children ten years old and younger. Perhaps

Socrates' tongue-in-cheek solution is simply intended to stop a tiresome discussion. But could he be demonstrating, as several scholars suggest, that political idealism is an absurd passion that leads to impractical suggestions and unreasonable conclusions? Or is he once more pointing out, in his ironic way, that the just city is an ideal model that can never be actualized, only approximated? And through this use of a shocking statement could Socrates merely be emphasizing the extreme importance of providing youth with a good, thorough education?

Whatever you decide, during your ventures into interpreting *The Republic* be certain to consider the crucial themes elaborated in this book—the place of education in the just society and the way in which moral character is shaped by intellect (reason).

# BOOK VIII: DEGENERATE SOCIETIES AND SOULS

Which life is the happier, the just or the unjust? This question guides the discussions of Books VIII and IX.

Book VIII begins with a brief review of the communal living arrangements of the guardians. Socrates then reminds his audience that although the just state has been described, other constitutions—defective ones—remain to be investigated. The point of the investigation is to demonstrate that happiness and injustice are incompatible.

In Book I Thrasymachus claimed that injustice brings happiness. Glaucon and Adeimantus carried on his argument (in the spirit of seeking clarity and not in the earnest conviction of belief) in Book II. At that time Socrates began his discourse on justice in the state and in the soul. And at the end of Book IV he was about to discuss the four kinds of injustices when

Polemarchus and Adeimantus interrupted, insisting on an in-depth account of the just state. Now, at last, through a comparison of just and unjust constitutions, Socrates plans to solve a practical issue—should youth follow Thrasymachus' advice and pursue injustice, or should they pursue justice?

The just state is an aristocracy. For Plato aristocracy means "the rule of the best people." Plato's aristocracy is the model constitution of the state and soul to which he compares other kinds of constitutions.

The pattern of the discussions on defective constitutions is similar to the pattern Plato used in Books III and IV. There he described justice in the state, followed by a direct comparison of justice in the state with justice in the soul. Here he explains how forms of government become corrupted, and then he reveals the corresponding corruption in the souls of individuals.

However, Plato includes a new twist in these discussions. The type of corruption of one generation of souls, he claims, is the result of the particular failings of the preceding generation. In other words, the father's sins are not only passed on to the son, but also cause the son to become even more degenerate than the father.

Plato's account of the progressive degeneracy of society is not based on actual historical or sociological evidence. It is a theoretical explanation of factors that contribute to people falling away from wisdom. And on another level it is a description of different types of personalities. For instance, at various points you may find yourself identifying with some of the desires and motivations of the degenerate souls Plato describes. Don't despair. Most people catch glimpses of some of their less admirable characteristics in these passages.

In this book (and continued in the next), Socrates discusses the following kinds of injustices found in states and in individuals: 1. timocracy; 2. oligarchy; 3. democracy; and 4. tyrrany.

## Timocracy (543a–550e)

Socrates' analysis of the relations among the five types of constitutions. He began with the perfect state, aristocracy, and now he proceeds to trace its decline from timocracy, to oligarchy, to democracy, and, finally, to the most wretched constitution, tyranny. He assumes that the best comes first. But he does recognize that there is a serious obstacle to the acceptance of his political theory of progressive degeneration: How can that which is perfect be susceptible to decay?

The just state, by definition, is perfect. And perfection, by definition, cannot undergo change because the term entails completeness, perpetual harmony, absence of destructive forces. Thus, Socrates has to show the presence of destructive forces where it would seem logical to assume that no destruction can occur.

Alas, even in the perfect state, somebody is going to make a mistake. The ideals of the intelligible world cannot long exist in the actual world of ever-changing events and of human passion. Socrates demonstrates how such mistakes come to pass by presenting a mathematical account of the proper times for "divine begettings." He says that all life forms are endowed with a predetermined cycle that somehow corresponds to the cycles of the heavenly bodies. These cycles, he says, can be mathematically calculated and known. Unfortunately, one day it will happen that the rulers of the perfect state will forget or ignore the proper cycles for human conception and beget children out of season. These indiscretions will lead to the decline of civilization. And the fall from aristocracy to degenerate forms of government and souls occurs, it turns out, because of poorly timed sex. Because of the rulers' failure to observe the cycle of divine begettings, iron people mix with silver and bronze people mix with gold (recall the Myth of the Metals in Book III). And the result is a less than perfect society—a timocracy.

But Socrates does not rely on the notion of the cycle of divine begettings alone to explain the eventual decay of the perfect state. He also says that political changes and revolutions occur when dissension arises within the ruling class. The inadequacies of and the quarrels among members of the ruling class often result in changes in governmental organization. The change from the rule of reason to the rule of emotion is the first change Socrates chronicles.

A timocracy is the rule of people who love honor (*timē* is Greek for "honor"). A timocratic state emerges when the auxiliaries, the high-spirited warriors of the just state, begin to usurp the power of the philosopher kings, the lovers of wisdom. The auxiliaries' love of honor engenders in them secret ambitions for power and wealth. Thus, when these warriors become the rulers of the state, they acquire personal possessions and maintain individual families. They begin neglecting their studies of the arts and sciences, and concentrate on physical training. And they don't educate future soldiers and rulers in dialectic (philosophy).

One name describes this first-level degenerate society—Sparta. Sparta had a form of government that Plato admired and it is his model for timocracy. It may have been less than a perfect state but, for Plato, it was as close to perfection as any existing state can become, except for one immensely major detail: Sparta did not encourage philosophy.

You may recall that Sparta defeated Athens in the Peloponnesian War. It was victorious in part because of its economic frugality, its intense discipline in the martial arts, and its internal loyalty and courage. Unlike democratic Athens, Sparta was ruled by a military elite who did not allow its citizens to accumulate wealth or to engage in unpatriotic cultural activities. Thus, Plato's timocratic state is not a bad place. The soldier-rulers like wealth, but they keep it in bounds and use it for state purposes. They are watchdogs of the state. You've heard of the Spartan life (one marked by thrift, simplicity, self-discipline, courage). That's what Plato means by a timocracy.

Also, that's what he means by the timocratic man. The constitution of the soul that corresponds to the timocratic state is Spartan through and through. The timocratic man has the marvelous attributes of loyalty, physical prowess, courage, and pride. But he is marred by being overly aggressive, secretly lustful for physical comforts, harsh toward underlings, fond of popular tunes, and not very articulate. The worst fault in the timocratic soul is the absence of reason as its ruler. The emotions rule. And, Socrates says, wisdom is not a part of the timocratic soul because physical training has been overemphasized.

How did the timocratic man come about? The timocratic youth, Socrates says, was probably the son of a good man living in a badly governed state. His father refused to get involved in the political intrigues and deceits of the state. (Could this man be Socrates who left a wife and children to pursue philosophy in the streets of Athens?) His mother, however, constantly quarreled with his father, telling the father that he should go after wealth and political power. The father disregarded his wife, ignored his son, and sought only his own counsel. In the meantime the mother raised the boy who decided to become a better man, in his mother's eyes, than his father. When the timocratic youth grew up, he sought honor, praise, and modest wealth. He became the timocratic man.

## Oligarchy (550c–555b)

An oligarchy, which literally means "government by the few," is a regime, Socrates says, based on a property qualification: The rich hold office and the poor are excluded. Because the timocratic rulers are secret lovers of wealth, they began accumulating treasure houses of gold and, eventually, wealth becomes the most honored thing in the state. Having a certain amount of money becomes the condition for holding political office; having an excellent character becomes a secondary consideration at best. Socrates compares the oligarchic state to a ship whose pilot is chosen on the basis of his wealth and not on his ability to navigate. Glaucon exclaims that a voyage on this ship would be a sorry one indeed!

The oligarchic state is divided against itself. It is, in effect, two cities—a city of the rich and a city of the poor. These two factions are constantly plotting against each other. Further, the citizens no longer know what their proper functions are in the state; they become meddlers and jacks-of-all-trades. Worse yet, after they have squandered their wealth they become either beggars (which Socrates compares to stingless bees) or criminals (stinger bees). The oligarchic state, thus, is marked by a lack of unity by dysfunction, and by crime.

The oligarchic youth is the son of a timocratic father who was mistreated by the people ("shipwrecked," Socrates says). The youth saw his father, a good man, lose his wealth and position in the state, perhaps even put to death, because of the deceit or excessive greed of other men. The son grows timid, loses his ambition, and, humbled by poverty, turns his efforts to the accumulation of wealth. He becomes stingy, unwilling to invest in things that could win him fame and honor. He hoards his money and soon finds himself rich. He is not a high-spirited man ruled by the emotion of conviction; rather, he is ruled by the love of money and the fear of losing his money. But he strives to maintain an honorable reputation and so becomes the man who seems just but is not altogether just (similar to Glaucon's Gyges in Book II). Yet he is not an unjust man either. Like the oligarchic state, the oligarchic man is plagued with internal dissension, he is constantly at war with himself. He is haunted by the spectre of poverty, and attracted to the glitter of gold.

## Democracy (555b–562a)

The word *democracy* literally means "the government of the people" (*demos*). Plato, of course, is using the term to refer to the democracy of Athens, a small city-state where every adult male citizen was a member of the Assembly, and so had a voice in governmental policy. But in Athens more than half of the population were slaves or foreign residents, neither of whom had any civic rights. Hence, the defects that Plato sees in Athenian democracy are probably not the same ones he would find in such modern-day democracies as the United States or France.

The transition from oligarchy to democracy results from the ever-growing conflict between the rich and the poor, which finally erupts into a civil war. The wealthy rulers of the oligarchy weaken themselves by their failure to check the economic extremes in the state. They become increasingly degenerate. Soon the poor masses find an opportunity to overthrow the soft, undisciplined rulers.

A democracy comes to be when the poor have gained control of the government. The poor execute or exile the oligarchs and grant the remaining citizens an equal share in policy-making and office-holding. Liberty and freedom of speech become the rule of the time. Each person may do as he pleases.

Socrates describes a democracy as a "bazaar of constitutions," a place where each man can select the type of life that pleases him. No one is forced to hold office, to serve in the military, to obey anyone else; and no one is considered to be better than anyone else. Further, a man who says he loves the people can get most anything he wants. With wry sarcasm (or is it?), Socrates says that the democracy seems to be "a delightful form of government, anarchic and motley, assigning a kind of equality indiscriminately to equals and unequals alike!"

Where, then, is the defect in the democratic constitution? Why does Plato consider a democracy a degenerate society that is only slightly more preferable than a tyranny?

Socrates reveals the defect when he describes the democratic man. He begins his description by distinguishing between necessary and unnecessary appetites. Appetites that maintain life are necessary; all others, and Socrates appears to include sex, are unnecessary. Although the oligarchic man loved wealth, he was ruled by his necessary appetites. Not so his son, who does not even respect wealth. The democratic youth seeks every kind of pleasure under the sun; his desires are unbridled by any concern for moderation. He neglects his studies and all honorable pursuits. He flaunts his appetites, for he believes that one pleasure is as good as another. As a democratic man he is unable to make distinctions. His total lack of a philosophical nature makes him a comic character whose life is merely a series of disorderly, meaningless pursuits. Plato's democratic man is the dilettante, the jet setter, the playboy, the common man whose life is founded on an unending quest for pleasure. One day his pleasure may be flute playing; the next, studying philosophy.

Unlike the other constitutions, the democratic state and man are not hostile to philosophy; they are simply indifferent. Plato's democracy is a "do your own thing" society. If your thing is to read philosophy, fine; if not, that's okay, too. Is Plato suggesting that philosophy is among the unnecessary desires?

---

**NOTE:** Plato's account of democracy is the strangest of his descriptions of the four degenerate constitutions. You may be left wondering if his discussion here is more of a defense of democracy than a condemnation. Certainly he praises timocracy as an orderly form of government, but he also appears to view democracy as advantageous to individuals. After all, if you want to devote your life to philosophical pursuits, in a democracy you can do so.

Some scholars suggest that Plato, rather than being antagonistic toward democracy, is actually defending democracy from its enemies—potential tyrants (powerful rulers unlimited by the laws of the people or by any constitution). What do you think? Do you think that Plato makes democracy the third kind of degeneracy because he wants to warn Athenians that their government can, in the blink of an eye, be turned into a tyranny? In other words, is he employing shock tactics to alert the people of Athens to the danger they are in of losing their freedom?

## Tyranny (562a–569c)

Democracy, Socrates says, degenerates into tyranny because of the excessive personal freedom permitted by the democratic leaders. A lack of respect for authority follows. Children have no awe or fear of their parents; teachers cater to the whims of their students; foreigners and slaves feel equal to citizens. "Things everywhere," Socrates says, "are just bursting with the spirit of liberty." Finally the democratic bubble bursts. Too much freedom brings anarchy; anarchy, in turn, brings the longing to be controlled.

The unlimited freedom of the democratic state divides people into three classes: the dominating class of spendthrift politicians, sycophants, and desperadoes; the capitalistic class of thrifty, wealthy businessmen; and the large mass of common people who own little property, keep quiet, and, for the most part, stay out of politics. The politicians begin to pass laws that affect the capitalists' wallets. The capitalists retaliate by forming a reactionary political party. Meanwhile, the masses feel the need for protection and elevate one man to champion their rights. This champion of the people tastes power, and, like a wolf that tastes blood, he becomes transformed into a dangerous creature, a tyrant. Power corrupts him.

At first the masses continue to believe that he is their friend. Some of the capitalists and politicians, however, perceive his considerable threat to the democracy and attempt to assassinate him. The budding tyrant demands that the people provide him with bodyguards. They do. And after a while he has acquired a close group of followers who are loyal only to him, and he has gained control of the state's army. He continually stirs up war with other states so that the people are always in need of a leader. Now the tyrant is firmly seated in power. He demands more and more of the people's property; taxes soar. But when the people protest, he has some of them killed and imprisons others. Soon the people realize that they have created a monster. But they are helpless; the tyrant has made the people his slaves.

With the tyrannical state established, Book VIII ends. A discussion on the tyrannical man begins the next book.

# BOOK IX: THE MISERABLE TYRANT

This book at last resolves the problems of justice raised by Thrasymachus at the close of Book I: Is justice more desirable than injustice in terms of happiness and profit?

In the last book Socrates launched his demonstration of the degeneration of society from aristocracy to tyranny. Here he shows the dismal depths the soul can reach. He compares such despair and personal enslavement with the delights of the philosophical life.

Book IX, then, completes the discussion on justice. In it Socrates explores three main topics: 1. the tyrannical man; 2. justice is happiness; and 3. justice is profitable.

## The Tyrannical Man (571a–576b)

Within the soul of each individual, Socrates says, there are tyrants. These tyrants are the unnecessary, lawless appetites that disturb our dreams. The healthy, sober individual, however, neither starves nor indulges his appetites. His appetitive part is lulled to sleep by reason as, also, is his passionate (emotional) part. On the other hand, the tyrannical man allows his beastly, savage part "to sally forth and satisfy its own instincts." But how does the tyrannical man come to be? What is the cause of his shameful, foul nature?

The democratic man, you will recall, was the son of the stingy, oligarchic man who disapproved of all unnecessary appetites, especially those whose object was entertainment. As a result the democratic man rebelled against his father's miserly ways and sought a compromise between moderation and indulgence. In a similar fashion the democratic son rebels against his father and pursues a life of uncontrolled appetites and passions.

Socrates describes the tyrannical man as a "monstrous winged drone" who has "madness for his bodyguard." He is a deranged man, drunken, lustful, maniacal. His appetites control his actions and lead him, if necessary, to rob and even kill his own parents if they stand in his way. No atrocity is beneath him. He will do anything to satisfy his appetites. He is the most enslaved man among men: He is enslaved from within. And the man who has the mightiest tyrant in his soul will most likely become the tyrant of the state.

## Justice Is Happiness (576b–588a)

Socrates claims that the tyrant is the most miserable of men. He attempts to prove this statement by advancing three different arguments: 1. the tyrant is actually a terrified slave (576c–580c); 2. the tyrant is not a judge of true pleasure (580d–583a); and 3. the tyrant cannot know pure pleasure (583b–588a).

**1.** Socrates introduces his first argument by referring Glaucon to the analogy between the state and the soul. He seeks to prove that the tyrannical state and soul are wretched, whereas the just state and soul are happy. The other types of constitutions fall, in various gradations, between the most miserable and the most happy. Also, Socrates gets Glaucon to agree that only a man ruled by reason—the philosopher—is capable of judging the best life from the worst. Now Socrates is ready to begin.

In a tyranny all people are enslaved, including the best men, the men of reason. Likewise, Socrates says, in the soul of the tyrant himself the best and most reasonable parts are enslaved, while the worst parts, the appetites, play the role of the tyrant and so are in control. Thus, the tyrant himself is tyrannized and is a slave to his appetites.

Moreover, the tyrant is utterly dependent on external things. This dependency fills him with fear and anxiety. For example, Socrates says to consider a wealthy citizen of Athens who owns many slaves. As long as he is protected by the laws of the state, he has nothing to fear. But suppose that suddenly he and his family are cast upon an island, outside of the law, with their fifty or more slaves. Will he not fear that the slaves will rise up against him? Will he not spend his days attempting to subdue his slaves through flattery and promises of freedom? Also, suppose the man becomes surrounded by neighbors who are opposed to slavery. He then finds that he is his slaves' slave and has no friends to help him.

In sum, this man's plight is the same as the tyrant's. The tyrant is unhappy in every way. He is surrounded by enemies from without (nobody likes a tyrant) and he is controlled by monstrous appetites and terrors from within.

2. Socrates' second argument is based on the tripartite soul: reason, emotion, appetite. According to Socrates each part of the soul has its own specific pleasure. Reason loves learning and wisdom; emotion loves victory and honor; appetite loves money and beautiful sensations. The characters of men also seem to fall into these three classes, so that the dominant love of an individual reveals the part of the soul that rules his personality. Each class of individuals naturally praises its own specific love as the most pleasurable.

However, the man who knows all three types of pleasure will be the best judge of which pleasure is the greatest. The philosopher is such a man. Further, the philosopher is in general best qualified to judge anything at all because he not only has *experience* of the three pleasures, but his experience is accompanied by *intelligence* and his judgments are informed by the art of *discussion*. Therefore, Socrates says, "the man of intelligence speaks with authority when he commends his own life," which, of course, is the life of learning and of philosophy. Socrates gives the life of honor second place and the life of money takes last place.

3.  The third and final argument turns on the distinction between the pure pleasures of the philosopher and the mixed pleasures of the tyrant. Socrates introduces his proof by revealing the conclusion he intends to reach: "Other pleasure than that of the intelligence is not altogether even real or pure, but is a kind of scene painting," is an illusion.

Pleasure and pain, most people say, are opposites. But Socrates notes that in between these extremes is a neutral state that he calls "quietude." When people are sick, they think that the highest pleasure is to be well. But when they are in good health, they are not aware of any particular pleasure of wellness. They are comfortable or at peace. Likewise, when delightful moments come to an end, pain is not experienced. There is quietude, a neutral state. Therefore, the absence of pain is not pleasure nor is the absence of pleasure pain.

Now, people without the philosopher's knowledge of truth and reality—and so inexperienced in true pleasure—believe that pleasure begins when pain ends. The fact is that these people, says Socrates, have experienced only pleasures of a shallow nature, of poor quality. And on the whole they are more accustomed to pain than to quietude. Thus when they move from pain to the neutral state, they believe that they are approaching true pleasure. In other words, for Socrates they are always in a state of becoming, they never reach true being or true pleasure. What is a true pleasure?

Socrates emphatically proclaims that the pleasures of sensation are not true pleasures. Eating, for example, ends hunger pains and it fills an emptiness. Eating seems pleasurable because hunger is painful. But like other sensual pleasures eating is not a positive, genuine pleasure. The true pleasures are those which fill the emptiness of the soul, not the body. These are the pleasures of knowledge.

In his uniquely paradoxical way, Socrates asks Glaucon:

> Then is not that which is fulfilled of what more truly is, and which itself more truly is, more truly filled and satisfied than that which being itself less real is filled with more unreal things? (585d)

Glaucon responds, "of course," although he probably wanted to ask, "Could you make that a little clearer?" Socrates is saying that the pleasures of the body are not true pleasures because the body itself—and all physical objects—is not real and eternal. Knowledge, however, is real, eternal, unchanging. Thus Socrates says to seek pleasure by feeding the mind. When the soul is guided by reason, by its wisdom-loving part, it is filled with true pleasure.

Because the tyrant is the man of slavish, sensual appetites, he of all people is the farthest removed from true pleasure. Here Socrates presents a mathematical proof on just how unhappy the tyrant is. Using a mathematical equation he shows that the philosopher is 729 times happier than the tyrant!

Socrates has finished his proofs on why the philosopher is the happiest of men and why the tyrant is the most miserable. The just life, after all, is the happy life. But Socrates never examines the notion of "happiness." You should, however, note that he makes the choice between the philosophic life and the tyrannic life depend on pleasure.

## Justice is Profitable (588b–592b)

This section completes the circle on the topic of justice begun in Book I. Socrates concludes that not only is the just life more profitable than the unjust, but also that it is better to be punished for wrongdoing than not.

Socrates employs "a symbolic image of the soul" for his proof on the considerable disadvantages of injustice. It goes like this: First image a many-headed beast that has a ring of tame and wild heads. Next image a lion and a man and join these with the beast. Enclose the three figures with an external shell that has the shape of a man. Now, what you have is an image of the tripartite soul.

Such men as Thrasymachus, who believe that injustice is profitable, appear to be saying that it is to one's advantage to nourish and to cater to the many-headed beast (the appetites, both necessary and unnecessary ones). But as the beast grows it drags the man wherever it will, it creates constant turmoil, and it devours the man from within. On the other hand, those men who affirm the profitable nature of justice give the man within the shell complete control over all parts of the soul. The internal man (reason) makes the lion (emotion) his ally and cares for the beast (appetite) in such a way that the beast is friendly and works for the good of the whole man.

Thus, being just—having harmonious unity within a soul guided by reason—is in a man's best interest. Analogously, the state ruled by philosopher kings is the happiest state and the best governed. Moreover, undetected and unpunished crimes feed the beast and starve reason. It is, therefore, in the wrongdoers' best interest to be punished lest the brutish part of the soul gains complete control.

At this point the compelling conflict of *The Republic* has been resolved. The proper choice between the philosophic and tyrannic lives should be clear. Even though the just man who is wrongly imprisoned or tortured cannot be happy, tyranny in the soul and state contains no element of happiness at all. The just life is profitable because justice is connected with self-sufficiency, self-esteem, and self-control.

This book ends with Socrates reasserting that the perfectly just state exists in theory only and is to be found nowhere on earth, now or ever. The just city, he says, is a pattern "laid up in heaven" for those people to follow who want to live the life of excellence.

# BOOK X: POETRY AND IMMORTALITY

This final book of *The Republic* serves as a kind of epilogue. Here Plato connects his criticism of poetry with his metaphysical Theory of Forms and with his psychology of the soul. He also demonstrates that the rewards of justice transcend the scope of this life and stretch on for eternity; the soul, he says, is immortal. These two topics seem to be unrelated. Yet Plato artistically brings criticism and immortality together through a comparison of Homeric poetry and Socratic poetry.

Book X begins with a somewhat surprising return to an earlier attack on old poetry and ends with an example of what new poetry must be. The book has two major sections: 1. poetry as the enemy of philosophy, and 2. the eternal rewards of justice.

## Poetry as the Enemy of Philosophy (595a–608b)

In Books II and III Plato demonstrated at length the harmful effects of the study of literature on future guardians. Why does he return to the subject of poetry now?

---

**NOTE:**     Recall that Plato's earlier attack on literature dealt only with its effects on the moral development of guardian children. He claimed that most literature encouraged the fear of death, disrespect for authority, acceptance of violence, and improper emotional behavior. Since that discussion, Plato has shared his world views on reality (especially in the Divided Line and the Allegory of the Cave) and on psychology (the tripartite soul). Now he can offer a more comprehensive attack on literature and can provide a philosophical basis for criticizing these educational materials of the Athenian youth.

In this section Plato doesn't simply criticize the content and the form of literature; he criticizes the major author, Homer. He seems to be saying, Out with Homer, in with Socrates. Most of the Athenians read and studied Homer, yet many of them mocked and condemned Socrates. Plato wants to defend Socrates and, in so doing, he singles out Homeric poetry as the enemy of Socratic philosophy, of dialectic.

---

Plato advances two attacks on poetry and the fine arts: 1. art is merely the imitation of the imitation of reality (595a–602b); and 2. the old poetry corrupts the soul (602c–608b).

Socrates begins his attack on poetry and the other arts (forms of imitation) with an apology. He says that although, like most Athenians, he has loved and respected Homer since he was a boy, a man must not be honored above the truth. And unfortunately Homer and other artists do not dwell on or convey truth. They are imitators. But what is wrong with imitation, especially such imitations as beautiful paintings and well-told stories? Socrates explains.

First he attempts to define *imitation*. He employs the concept of a couch as his example. There are, of course, many couches made by craftsmen. But the craftsmen did not make the idea of "couch"; they simply build the many couches that participate in the *one* idea (form) of couch, which was first conceived by the Great Craftsman, the creator of all ideas. Thus, the furniture makers are twice removed from the reality of couch. They neither created the idea nor are they the physical couch itself.

Now, artists who paint pictures of couches are three times removed from the reality of couch because they produce no more than a representation (image) of the appearance (physical object) of the idea (reality). In other words, you cannot sit on the couch in a painting, you learn almost nothing about three-dimensional couches by looking at a painting, and the artist gives you no insight on the *one* idea of couch. Therefore, artistic imagination is on the bottom level of intellectual experience. And so, for Socrates imitation has no educational value because, as you will recall from the Divided Line and the Allegory of the Cave, the things on the bottom level do not have the power to spur intellectual growth and are not conducive to learning.

Yet artists, at least according to Socrates, have an even worse failing than perpetuating fantasy. Socrates accuses them of being ignorant braggarts. Artists claim to be, or are reputed to be, knowledgeable about all of the arts and sciences and everything else under the sun. Such claims make artists the opponents of philosophy. Artists claim to have knowledge that they do not have. And they are dangerous because they have the ability to seduce people into believing them. They are flatterers, seekers of public approval, and emotional con men.

Socrates rhetorically speaks to Homer. He asks: What are the benefits of your art? Does your poetry help people to live better lives? He then lists, in an ascending order of importance, the functions Homer never performed but that, in his poetic way, he claimed to be able to perform in his imitative writing (that is, in his pretense to be people other than himself): a politician, general, businessman, teacher, and philosopher. Socrates denounces Homer's pretense and says that "all of the poetic tribe, beginning with Homer, are imitators of images of excellence." He claims that if artists were able to portray "reality," they would abandon their games—their form of play that must not be taken seriously—and become involved in such activities as statesmanship and education, areas of the state where character is developed and where intellect rules.

---

**NOTE:**    As you see here and as you've seen before, for Plato human excellence is performing the highest function of human capabilities well. Excellence is acting in accordance with reason. Artists to him are playful creatures who serve no significant function but who, nevertheless, are taken quite seriously by the "ignorant multitude." Their impact on people's emotions and beliefs make them extremely dangerous to the well-being of the state and soul.

Plato's criticism of the arts raises many significant questions about the purpose and place of art in society. For example: What is "art"? What are the values of aesthetic experience? Are artists frauds who pretend to have wisdom? Can literature and the visual arts influence youth to pursue the life of reason? Should literature and the fine arts be excluded from educational programs? Does, as Plato suggests in the next section, life imitate art?

---

Plato seems unduly harsh on poetry and poets. His criticism, although interesting and thought-provoking, seems to neglect a look at one of the purposes of art of which even he would approve—to inspire a higher vision of life. Moreover, the criticism he leveled

at Homer in the last argument—that Homer was neither a statesman nor a teacher of mathematics—
equally applies to Socrates.

In this second strand of the criticism Plato's vendet-
ta against the poets, Homer in particular, has Plato
attempting to prove that no place for poets exists in
the perfectly just state. Poets must either leave the
state or stop being poets or change the subjects on
which they write. Why? Because their works, as they
stand, corrupt the souls of the populace.

Socrates begins the second attack by demonstrating
that poetry, because it is imitation and illusion,
appeals to the part of the soul that is "remote from
intelligence," and so fosters inferior thoughts and
emotions. Socrates uses an example of a man grieving
over the loss of his son. When he is alone the grieving
man vents his feelings in loud, woeful utterances. But
in the public view he resists his impulses toward
uncontrolled despair and maintains the demeanor of
a reasonable man. Poets, Socrates says, choose to portray the private moments of life, for instance, the
stricken man's wailing and writhing. One reason for
this is that the "fretful part" of the soul is the easiest to
imitate and is most readily understood by the "non-
descript mob in the theater." On the other hand, the
rational man, leading an orderly and just life, is hard
to portray in art and does not seem to interest an audience. Thus, through art, people are moved by dis-
plays of emotion that they would be ashamed to
reveal publicly.

Socrates implies that life imitates art: "For after feeding fat the emotion of pity there [in the theater], it is
not easy to restrain it in our own suffering." Nor is
pity the only emotion that we are prone to imitate. We
see buffoons and play the clown ourselves, with the

emotions of anger and lust. He proclaims that poetic imitation

> waters and fosters these feelings when what we ought to do is to dry them up, and it establishes them as our rulers when they ought to be ruled, to the end that we may be better and happier men instead of worse and more miserable. (606d)

Therefore, although Homer is the greatest of poets, even his poems cannot be admitted to the city. The only acceptable poems are hymns to the gods and the praises of good men. All other poetry is the enemy of philosophy because it strengthens the emotions that war with reason. Tyrants praise appetite. Poets praise emotion. Philosophers praise reason, so only they can be permitted to educate youth and to influence the masses.

Although here Socrates banishes poetry from the city, he offers it a return when it can show itself to be a friend of philosophy, that is, when it realizes that its function is to subordinate emotion to reason and not, as it now does, to overwhelm reason with emotion.

## The Eternal Rewards of Justice (608c–end)

The previous discussion on poetry is, in part, a preparation for a discussion on immortality and the rewards of justice. The Myth of Er, which ends *The Republic*, is more poetic than it is philosophic. And the arguments that lead to this poetic finale lack the philosophic rigor that characterizes most of Socrates' arguments. More than anything else, here Socrates appears to be praising justice. He ends the discussion at Cephalus' home by presenting his ode to justice.

This section can be divided into three parts: 1. a proof of immortality (608c–612a); 2. the rewards of justice in this life (612a–613e); and 3. the Myth of Er (613e–end).

**1.** Socrates surprises Glaucon by declaring his belief in the immortality of the soul. Whether Socrates actually believed in personal immortality is a matter of conjecture. But because the study of eternal ideas is the proper study of man, he investigates the possibility of the eternal existence of the human soul. This argument, however, can hardly be termed a "proof." Rather, it is a venture into a logical examination of how the words *good* and *evil* are used in relation to the human body and character. Its goal seems to be to persuade you that in the final analysis justice has its rewards.

The argument goes like this: Evil is that which destroys and corrupts; good is that which preserves and benefits. And everything has its special good and evil. For example, certain chemicals preserve wood, and certain grain mildew destroys it. Proper nutrition preserves the human body, and disease destroys it. The soul also has its goods and evils. Injustice, as Socrates has gone to great lengths to point out, is the special evil of the soul. Yet tyrants and other unjust people do not seem to be destroyed by injustice. They often continue to thrive until ripe old age. Therefore, if the soul cannot be destroyed by its particular evil, then it cannot be destroyed at all and, so, must be immortal.

---

**NOTE:** As you see, this proof is not a compelling one. Unjust men do not have early deaths—so what? Does this prove anything beyond the cliché that life isn't always fair? Further, this "proof" does not commit Socrates to a belief in individual immortality, but simply to a belief in some form of immortality, which is probably the immortality of such ideas as justice and injustice.

---

**2.** Glaucon says that if injustice is not fatal to its possessor, then injustice does not seem to be such a terrible thing. And, worse yet, injustice, as well as justice, will exist forever.

Socrates does not contradict Glaucon. Instead, at this point he strives to convince Glaucon that justice has its rewards in this life. Here Socrates does not actually present an argument. For one thing, the reasons for being just cannot depend on the external benefits that justice may bestow on man. Justice is good in and by itself. It is the health of the soul, and health of any kind is valuable for its own sake. But the nice thing is that experience shows that most people tend to reward just actions and believe that honesty is the best policy. Thus, Socrates concludes, a man ought to behave justly whether he possesses the ring of Gyges or not.

**3.** The Myth of Er is a Socratic poem in praise of justice. It is fitting for Socrates, the man of many images, to end his discussion on justice with an extended image of the eternal value of living a philosophical life.

Er was a bold warrior who was slain in battle. His body was found among the decaying corpses ten days later, yet still in good shape. When his body was taken home and put on the funeral pyre, he came back to life. And he told the following story of his adventures in the other world.

After his soul left his body, Er journeyed with the other departed souls to a mysterious region where there were two openings in the earth and two corresponding openings in heaven. In that place the souls were judged. Some were sent to heaven; others into the bowels of the earth. Er, however, was not judged. He was told that he had been chosen to witness the proceedings of the souls to and from life and to return to his friends to tell what he had seen.

Not only were there souls going into the upper and lower regions, but there were souls coming out of the openings of both heaven and earth. As Er stood by he heard some of the stories of the arriving souls, of those who were about to be reincarnated. By listening to them and by following them on their journey to the land of Necessity where they would choose their next lives, Er learned about the mysteries of immortality.

Those dusty and squalid souls coming out of the earth wailed about their horrible experiences. Those clean and pure souls coming from heaven related delights and visions of beauty beyond words. However, at the mouth of the earthen arrival gate there were souls wailing to be released. They were hurled back into the tortures of the underworld. These souls were the incurably wicked whose great crimes against humanity may never be paid, their souls never purged.

All souls that had emerged from the openings, both the punished and the rewarded, gladly assembled in a meadow waiting for their next assignment on earth. They were, no doubt, ready for a change because they had been away from life for a thousand years and had experienced pleasure or pain ten times as strong as their past-life deeds had brought to others.

After seven days in the meadow the group destined for rebirth journeyed to the spindle of Necessity. Here the three Fates (past, present, and future) distributed lots to the souls soon to be mortals. The lots designated the order in which the souls would choose their next lives. Then the Fates flung the patterns of lives, much more numerous than the assembled souls, onto the ground. Every sort of animal and human life was represented, from tyrants to apes, from the average man to eagles.

Each soul got to choose his future existence. The one who had drawn the first lot chose to be a tyrant. He was an ignorant soul who, having lived all these centuries in heaven, wanted to taste power and luxury. But he soon discovered that he would engage in such despicable deeds as eating his own children. Another soul chose to be a swan because he was still feeling the pains of human life. And on and on. Some souls chose wisely, others foolishly, but in most cases the souls made their choices on the basis of their past lives. Those who had led a life of justice and knowledge were best equipped to choose a happy life to come.

This, then, is the moral of Socrates' tales: By pursuing a life of wisdom, you ensure your chances of living harmoniously and happily forever. The pleasures of the body come and go, but wisdom is eternal and is eternally beneficial.

Another moral is that there is no one to blame but yourself for the life you lead. Each person is responsible for the course of his life. People who have knowledge realize this universal law and know that justice is both its own reward and the blessing of the ages.

The Myth of Er reveals Socrates' view that people are fully responsible for the lives they lead and that not to accept the responsibility for learning more about such eternal ideas as the principle of justice and the path of human excellence is ignorance.

Justice has been revealed and rewarded. The Socratic poem has been told. And *The Republic* is ended.

# A STEP BEYOND

## Tests and Answers

### TESTS

### Test 1

1. Two of the speakers taking part in Plato's _____
   dialogues are his brothers,
   A. Glaucon and Adeimantus
   B. Polemarchus and Bendis
   C. Cephalus and Philemon

2. Thrasymachus is the speaker _____
   A. most easily demolished by Socrates
   B. who is the most formidable adversary for
      Socrates
   C. who wins grudging approval from
      Socrates

3. In the opening argument we learn that _____
   riches
   A. encourage you to want even more
   B. make it easier for you to do what is right
   C. are the undoing of many men

4. Benefiting your friends and causing harm to _____
   your enemies is Polemarchus' definition of
   A. good sense
   B. expedience
   C. justice

5. A Socratic conclusion is that
   I. it is never right to do evil to anyone
   II. the only way to harm a man is by
       making him a worse man

       III. it is sometimes right to refuse to
           obey a ruler
    A. I and II only
    B. II and III only
    C. I, II, and III

6. Which type of argument is *not* a Socratic     \_\_\_\_\_
technique?
    A. analogy
    B. parable
    C. statistics

7. A well-known theory promulgated by one of     \_\_\_\_\_
the speakers is
    A. The End Justifies The Means
    B. Might Makes Right
    C. Each Man's Reach Must Exceed His
       Grasp

8. A clever argument put forth by Glaucon is     \_\_\_\_\_
that
    A. it is ridiculous to think that an unjust man
       is happier than a just one
    B. only a fool would choose to be unjust in a
       just society
    C. it is much better to seem to be just than
       actually to be just

9. Which of these examples is *not* offered by     \_\_\_\_\_
Socrates?
    A. the violent man with the carving knife
    B. the carpenter who lacks the proper tools
    C. the Allegory of the Cave

10. Another Platonic description for soldiers is     \_\_\_\_\_
    A. warrior kings
    B. vigilant ones
    C. guardians

11. Describe the Socratic method—sometimes called the Method of Dialectic—and illustrate it with an example from *The Republic*.

12. Plato is not only a philosopher, he is also an artist who brings literary expression to his ideas. Discuss Plato's artistry in *The Republic*.

13. Trace Plato's examination of the nature of justice from the introduction of the topic in Book I to the discovery of justice in the soul in Book IV.

## Test 2

1. In Plato's ideal state children would be          _____
   A. shielded from evil
   B. taught to speak up for their rights
   C. kept out of formal schooling until the age
      of eight

2. The three classes of citizens in Plato's ideal    _____
   state are
   A. rulers, followers, and philosophers
   B. rulers, auxiliaries, and craftsmen
   C. rulers, functionaries, and poets

3. Socrates proposed the Myth of Metals to           _____
   A. ensure communal stability
   B. justify the classless society
   C. explain why the soldiers were entitled to
      the obedience of others

4. In a smooth-functioning state, Socrates           _____
   argued,
   A. only a few laws would be required
   B. some extremes can be tolerated
   C. periodic wars need not paralyze society

5. The Four Cardinal Virtues mentioned in *The*      _____
   *Republic* are justice, wisdom, courage, and
   A. love
   B. discipline
   C. piety

6. The three divisions of the mind, according to     _____
   Socrates, are reason, the emotional part, and
   A. desire
   B. quiet contemplation
   C. conscience

7. According to Plato, since the object of _____
   knowledge is beauty, then
   A. hedonism must be shunned at all costs
   B. only a truly wise man can succeed as a poet
      philosopher
   C. beauty must really exist

8. Socrates' famous story of the cave makes the
   point that
        I. all knowledge is connected
       II. philosophers must apply what
          they have learned
       III. the shadows on the cave's wall may
          be the real thing
   A. I and II only
   B. II and III only
   C. I, II, and III

9. Timocracy, oligarchy, democracy, and tyranny _____
   are described as four types of
   A. states with potential for good
   B. unjust societies
   C. governments that are worthy of partial
      admiration

10. The point of the Myth of Er is that _____
    A. we are responsible for the lives we choose
       to lead
    B. we are the victims of our fate
    C. virtue is its own reward

11. The Analogy of the Sun, the Divided Line, and the Alle-
    gory of the Cave are three related images. Describe their
    connection and briefly discuss their significance to the
    topic of justice.

12. What is a philosopher according to Plato? Why should philosophers be kings?

13. How do the philosopher and tyrant differ? Note their differences in terms of the tripartite soul and also include the ways in which the images of the Divided Line and the Allegory of the Cave can inform your judgment on their differences.

# ANSWERS

## Test 1

**1.** A    **2.** A    **3.** B    **4.** C    **5.** C    **6.** C
**7.** B    **8.** C    **9.** B    **10.** C

**11.** The Socratic method, thought to be invented by Socrates and employed by Plato in many of his dialogues, is a form of argumentation that seeks knowledge (usually definitions of such abstract concepts as justice and virtue) by a process of question and answer. In Book VII Plato refers to this method as *dialectic*. He describes dialectic as the systematic inquiry into the true nature of things by asking and answering questions in a logically rigorous manner (533a–d).

The purpose of the method is to reveal the significance and truth of such claims as "justice is telling the truth and paying one's debts" (330d–331d) and "justice is to the advantage of the stronger" (336b–347e). When the method is successful, it culminates in the questioner (usually Socrates) catching the answerer in a contradiction or in an argumentative impasse. An impasse occurs when the answerer sees the problems with or the errors in his thinking and sees that he can progress no farther in the argument until he redefines his terms or even denies his original claim. Thus, the method is often used to arrive at the starting point of a philosophical discussion rather than simply determining *the* answer. Ideally, however, the answerer can find a way out of the impasse and discover a truth.

For example, in Book IX Socrates uses the process of dialectic to prove that philosophers, not tyrants, have true pleasure. First he presents two concepts that seem to be in conflict—pleasure and pain. Then he demonstrates that although pleasure and pain are opposites, they are not really in conflict because, for instance, the riddance of pain is not pleasure but is a neutral state intermediate between pleasure and pain. Thus, the so-called pleasures that tyrants seek—the fulfillment of bodily appetites—are merely relief from such pain as hunger or thirst.

At this point Socrates has presented a potential conflict and has reached an impasse—pleasure cannot be the satisfaction of bodily desires. He then proceeds to demonstrate what true pleasure is.

Other examples of dialectic are found throughout *The Republic*, but perhaps the best are in Book I, beginning with the simple discussion with Cephalus and moving to the more complex argument with Thrasymachus on the profitable nature of injustice.

**12.** For centuries Plato has inspired people to imagine their own vision of the Good Life. His success as an artist philosopher stems in part from his dramatic presentations of provocative ideas. Through the use of dialogue and poetic images he has stimulated others to examine the nature of reality and human life with both intellectual seriousness and playfulness.

As an artistic form, dialogue permits Plato to demonstrate the movement of an argument. Dialogues are conversations between two or more characters and, as conversations, they exhibit the liveliness of intellectual discovery. For instance, Socrates claims that he does not know what "justice" is, but he says, after some prodding from his young friends Glaucon and Adeimantus, that he is willing to explore the nature of justice. What ensues is an intellectually exciting conversation, with Socrates as the main speaker, that takes many turns, has a few detours, but ultimately leads to a vision of the perfectly just state. If Plato had simply written a treatise on the nature of justice we would have been denied the pleasure of witnessing a keen mind in the process of seeking understanding and of creating a dramatic picture of life in an "ideal" society.

Further, Plato enlivens his presentation of justice by providing vivid images that illustrate his ideas more clearly than argument alone could do. For example, the Myth of the Metals (414c–416c) sets up an image for discussing the nature-nurture problem. The Parable of the Ship of State (488a–489c) reveals the "useless" position of philosophers in a state devoted to political struggle and intrigue. The Analogy of the Sun (506e–509c) brings to light the distinction between sensible and intelligible objects. The Divided Line (509c–511e) and the Allegory of the Cave (514a–621b) show us the ascending scale of reality and intellectual development. And the Myth of Er (613e–end) presents a speculative view of the eternal rewards of justice. Thus, Plato is both a philosopher and a poet. His artistry offers us intellectual vision coupled with dramatic insight and inspiration.

**13.** In Book I Cephalus says that justice is telling the truth and paying one's debts. His son Polemarchus adds that justice is giving every man his due, which he interprets to mean that justice is what benefits one's friends and harms one's enemies. Socrates, through the process of dialectic, demonstrates that both of these views on justice are inadequate.

Thrasymachus bursts into the discussion and presents an argument that goes against the grain of traditional morality. He insists that justice is to the advantage of the stronger; in other words, justice is whatever the rulers of a state say it is. He also claims that it is more profitable for an individual to be unjust than to be just. Socrates counters Thrasymachus' arguments, succeeds in quieting him, but admits that what justice really is has still not been determined.

In Book II Glaucon and Adeimantus demand that Socrates prove to them that it is better to lead a just life than an unjust one. They want to be shown that living justly is the best way to live regardless of any financial rewards or of the good reputation that can result from just behavior. Socrates complies with their wishes and, with their help, sets out to examine what justice is in itself and by itself.

He begins by constructing the just city for, as he says, it takes keen vision to see justice in the soul. First, justice must be "writ large," that is, must be revealed in the operations of an ideal city-state. He proceeds by creating a city that is divided into three classes—rulers, auxiliaries, and producers. Most of Book III is concerned with the education of the guardians (future rulers and auxiliaries).

In Book IV Socrates discovers the particular function and excellence of each class. Rulers govern and must have reason; auxiliaries protect and must have courage; and producers take care of physical needs and must have moderation. But where is justice? Socrates says that justice is the harmonious functioning of all of the members of the city; it is each class performing its tasks well and not meddling in the affairs of the other classes.

Likewise, in the souls of men, justice is the harmonizing of the various parts of the soul. Reason (wisdom) must always govern and ally itself with emotion (courage and conviction). And both reason and emotion must control desire (the moderation of the base appetites and emotions). Thus, justice in both the city and the soul is the health produced by the harmonious functioning of intelligence, spiritedness, and bodily sensation.

## Test 2

1. A    2. B    3. A    4. A    5. B    6. A
7. C    8. A    9. B    10. A

**11.** In Books VI and VII of *The Republic* Plato uses three images to explain his theory of knowledge and to demonstrate the educational steps one must take in order to have knowledge of reality.

The Analogy of the Sun is the first and simplest image. Here Socrates distinguishes between visible and intelligible objects. He compares the light of the sun, by which we are able to see the actual things of the world, to the sun itself, which is the source of things being visible. Like the sun, the idea of the good is the source of things being intelligible; it is the source of all ideas. And reason is the faculty of the mind that grasps ideas. Thus the sun is to seeing as the idea of the good is to reasoning.

The Divided Line explains the distinction between the sensible and the intelligible more fully. The visible world of things that we daily come in contact with are shadows/reflections of physical objects and the physical objects themselves. But to trúly understand the physical objects and events of the actual world, we must grasp the intelligible ideas on which they depend; the ideas give physical objects meaning and essence. Ideas are intelligible objects and are divided by Plato into the objects of mathematics (for example, the concept of a circle) and into the forms (the highest principles and theories that inform us about the greatest function and the greatest knowledge of mankind—the Good Life and the ultimate purpose of all things).

After presenting this blueprint of the realms of knowledge, Plato puts his theory of knowledge and education into a poetic form, which is sometimes called the Allegory of the

Cave. This cave image is the story of a man's ascent from the subterranean depths of ignorance, from thinking that shadows of sensible objects are reality, to his revelation in the sun of the cause and purpose of all things, of the reality of the good and of how things are and ought to be for all mankind, including the other people in the cave below.

What do these images on knowledge and reality have to do with the concept of justice? "Justice" is, of course, an intelligible object and is one of the principal components that comprise the highest idea, the form of the good. To truly understand justice, one must understand the Good Life and the harmonious functioning that is necessary for true pleasure to be achieved in society and in the individual soul. Is such understanding an impossible goal? Maybe. But Socrates claims to offer only a vision of the ideal. And the three images that Plato has him present make the ideal more vivid.

12. For Plato, Socrates is the model philosopher and the model for potential philosophers. Socrates is a lover of wisdom and a seeker of truth. He is not dogmatic in his beliefs; rather, he continually questions other people on their beliefs. He scrutinizes the statements of others with an intense, unrelenting logic. In *The Republic* Socrates plays two roles: the role of examiner of others' beliefs, especially in Book I, and the role of the wise man. In the latter role he puts forth his own ideas for the scrutiny of others (or perhaps he puts forth the ideas that Plato garnered from his tutelage with Socrates and that Plato embellished as a result of his own experience and insight). Among the issues that the philosopher Socrates discusses in *The Republic* are the characteristics of philosophers, their proper activities, and their rightful place in society.

After constructing the just state, in Book V Socrates says that until philosophers become kings and kings become philosophers the troubles of society and of individual souls will continue. But why should philosophers become kings? What attributes do they have that present politicians do not have?

Socrates compares the true philosopher to the amateur. Spectacles of all kinds—Dionysian festivals and other exotic gatherings of people—fascinate amateur philosophers. Amateurs, thus, are not as interested in discovering universal truths as they are in absorbing the particular, exciting sensations of the moment. On the other hand, true philosophers ignore momentary intrigues and keep their intellectual sights aimed at the understanding of eternal, unchanging knowledge. True philosophers are tireless scholars who have an incorruptible moral character. This combination of wisdom and virtue makes them the ideal candidates for rulers of the state.

But, alas, in Book VI Socrates says that the philosopher is considered useless in present societies and in fact is useless. Philosophers have neither the character for nor the interest in engaging in the political frays—often deceitful, underhanded, and demeaning—that seem to be required of men who succeed in acquiring power. What, then, is to be done? How is it possible for philosophers to be kings?

In Book VII Socrates outlines a total educational program for gifted youth who have the potential for becoming the "true pilots" of the state. The potential philosopher kings will be physically well trained, will spend ten years studying mathematics and related sciences, and will spend five years studying dialectic (the art of systematically inquiring into the nature of reality—philosophy, Socrates' art). They will follow their fifteen years of higher education with a fifteen-year internship in the practical workings of the state (in other words, they will return to the cave of illusion, but with insight and purpose). At the age of fifty the best of the best will become the philosopher kings and will govern the state with wisdom and virtue, both attributes backed by a solid foundation of practical experience. These rulers will be the embodiment of the just state—ruled by reason and characterized by harmony between their emotions and desires and between their personalities and the rest of society.

The perfectly just state, therefore, will be ruled by philosophers, that is, by people who are exceptionally well educated, have vast practical wisdom of government and society, and have justice within their souls.

**13.**    Philosophers are lovers of wisdom, seekers of truth. And according to Plato philosophers should be rulers of the state, even though they have no desire to rule. What they do have is the knowledge and moral character necessary for excellent leadership.

Tyrants, on the other hand, are lovers of base pleasures and of tremendous wealth. They are all-powerful rulers who seek their own advantage instead of looking after the health of the state and the welfare of the people they rule. What they lack is reason and moral character. They are unhealthy people, in both body and soul, because they are enslaved by their appetites, which in turn causes them to enslave the people (their subjects) who are forced to cater to the tyrants' appetites.

Thus philosophers and tyrants represent the two extremes of moral character. Using the model of the tripartite soul, we can better understand the differences between the philosopher and tyrant. The soul of the philosopher is guided by reason. His greatest pleasure is learning. The soul of the tyrant is guided by his appetites. His greatest pleasure is to be physically satisfied, for example, sated by food and wine and surrounded by silk and gold.

Despite his wealth and power, the tyrant is the most miserable of men, says Socrates, because he is despised by all others and is devoured from within. He knows no true pleasure or happiness. Only people with a philosophic nature can have true pleasure; they are continually filling their souls with knowledge which, unlike physical appetite, never admits of emptiness.

In the Allegory of the Cave philosophers are those people who escape from the chains of ignorance and through an extended and rigorous educational process ascend the cave path and emerge in the light of the sun, into the knowledge of reality. That is, the philosopher moves from level 1 of the Divided Line (being aware of shadows and reflections of imitations of reality) to level 4 (having knowledge of universal principles and of the form of the good). Tyrants, however, spend their lives in the cave grasping shadows. They never experience the pleasures of true knowledge and so always remain more enslaved (chained to passion) than the people they enslave.

# Term Paper Ideas

1. What are the similarities and differences of justice in the individual and justice in the state. Be certain to discuss the differences between politics and psychology.

2. In Book I Socrates tells Polemarchus that justice cannot be anything that is injurious to the soul. What does this argument tell you about Socrates' notion on punishment? What is the difference between justice and punishment?

3. What does Socrates mean by "happiness"? Why does he distinguish happiness in the individual from happiness in the state?

4. According to Socrates, what is a philosopher? Does Plato's description of the character and role of a philosopher differ from today's?

5. Discuss the benefits and disadvantages of each class in the just society. What do you think of a "class society"?

6. Should philosophers be kings? Discuss Socrates' view on this issue and agree or disagree with him.

7. Discuss Plato's view of the significance and place of wealth in society.

8. Why should people be just? There are obvious advantages to a government for people to be just, but what are the advantages to the individual?

9. List the ways in which potential scholars are corrupted by society and, as a result, turn away from philosophy. Provide several other ways in which students can be seduced away from their studies.

10. Summarize Plato's reasons for censoring certain poetry and other art works. Do you think his reasons are valid?

**11.** What do you think of Plato's treatment of the problem of the equality of women?

**12.** What does Socrates mean by "true pleasure"? How does it differ from other types of pleasure? How does one acquire true pleasure?

**13.** Plato believes that knowledge for its own sake is enough justification for devoting one's life to studying and learning. Agree or disagree.

**14.** Discuss the relationship between the Divided Line and the Allegory of the Cave.

**15.** Does art imitate life or does life imitate art? Is *The Republic* a work of art or of science or of something else?

# Further Reading

## CRITICAL WORKS

Jaeger, Werner. *Paideia: The Ideals of Greek Culture*, vols. II and III. (trans. Gilbert Highet.) New York: Oxford University Press, 1943.

Koyre, Alexandre. *Discovering Plato.* (trans. Leonora Cohen Rosenfield). New York: Columbia University Press, 1945.

Lavine, T. Z. *From Socrates to Sartre: The Philosophic Quest.* New York: Bantam Books, 1984.

Randall, John Herman. *Plato: Dramatist of the Life of Reason.* New York: Columbia University Press, 1970.

Ryle, Gilbert. *Plato's Progress*. London: Cambridge University Press, 1966.

Taylor, A. E. *Plato: The Man and His Work*. London: Methuen & Co., 1966.

## SELECTED TRANSLATIONS OF *THE REPUBLIC*

Bloom, Allan. *The Republic of Plato*. New York: Basic Books, 1968. A literal translation supplemented with extensive notes and an interpretive essay.

Cornford, Francis MacDonald. *The Republic of Plato*. New York: Oxford University Press, 1956. A translation that includes summaries before each major section and has frequent footnotes.

Davies, John Llewelyn, and David James Vaughan. *The Republic of Plato*. New York: A. L. Burt, 1900. A literal translation with an introductory, analytical essay.

Grube, G. M. A. *Plato: The Republic*. Indianapolis: Hacket, 1974. A literal translation with introductory comments before each book, and with footnotes.

Lee, H. D. P. *Plato: The Republic*. Baltimore: Penguin, 1955. A translation rendered when appropriate in the modern idiom. Includes an introductory essay and summaries before each major section.

Shorey, Paul. *Plato: The Republic*. Cambridge, Mass.: Loeb Classical Library, 1930. A literal translation reprinted in *The Collected Dialogues of Plato*, ed. Edith Hamilton and Huntington Cairns. New York: Pantheon Books, 1964.

# AUTHOR'S SELECTED WORKS

## Earlier Dialogues

*Gorgias*
*Protagoras*
*Meno*
*Euthyphro*
*The Apology*
*Crito*
*Phaedo*
*Symposium*
*Phaedrus*
*The Republic*
*Parmenides*
*Theaetetus*

# Later Dialogues

*Sophist*
*Statesman*
*Philebus*
*Timaeus*
*Laws*

# Glossary

**Agora**  The marketplace of ancient Greece and the central meeting place in the city.

**Allegory**  An expression, usually in the form of a story, intended to convey a truth or generalization about the human condition through the use of symbolic characters and objects—for example, Plato's Allegory of the Cave.

**Delphic Oracle**  The prophet (seer) of the temple of Apollo at Delphi who the ancient Greeks believed had the power to foretell the future and who was consulted when important decisions had to be made. The temple in which the oracle dwelled was reputed to be at the center (the navel) of the earth.

**Dialectic**  A term Plato uses to designate the process of moving from hypothetical starting points (some of which often seem to conflict or to be contradictory) of arguments to first principles of the nature of things. For Plato, the terms "dialectic" and "philosophy" are usually synonymous.

**Epistemology**  A major discipline of philosophy that investigates the nature, limitations, scope, and sources of knowledge. In the Greek language *episteme* means "knowledge" or "science" and *logos* means, among other things, "theory" and "study"; thus, epistemology is the study of knowledge.

**Eros**  A Greek word meaning "love," usually sensual, erotic love. Also, Eros is the name of the Greek god of love, the son of Aphrodite.

**Ethos**  The Greek word meaning "character" or "custom" from which we derive the word "ethics" (the discipline that deals with moral values, principles, and character traits).

**Fates**  Three Greek goddesses, the daughters of Necessity; Lachesis holds sway over the past, Clotho over the present, and Atropos over the future.

**Hoi polloi**  A Greek term meaning "the many" and often translated as "the multitude," "the mob," "the vulgar masses," and "the common people."

**Hypothesis**  A tentative assumption or a formulation of a general principle based on inference from observed data. Plato includes hypotheses in level 3 of the Divided Line; thus, for him, hypotheses are the objects of knowledge derived from reflection on the nature of the physical world.

**Muses**  The nine sister goddesses of Greek mythology who presided over the various arts—music, history, visual arts, literature, culture, philosophy.

**Paradigm**  A theoretical model or pattern; Plato's Divided Line, for example, presents a theoretical model of the ascending levels of having knowledge.

**Polis**  The Greek word for "city," "city-state," or "state"; the word from which we derive the word "politics" (the discipline that deals with governmental policy and organization).

**Pythagoreans**  Groups of men and women who, in Plato's time, formed secret cults devoted to the study of mathematics, music, and philosophy. It is supposed that a man called Pythagoras, who probably lived during the sixth century B.C. yet whom we know almost nothing about, combined ideas on mathematics and mysticism and was the inspiration for the later Pythagorean mystery cults.

**Socratic method**     Another name for the method of dialectic [see *Dialectic* and the Note in Book I, section 2].

**Sophists**     Traveling lecturers and teachers who went from city to city teaching young men the art of public speaking (rhetoric) and the art of practical politics.

# NOTES

**DATE DUE**

| | | | |
|---|---|---|---|
| FE 6 87 | | | |
| MR 20 87 | | | |
| JA 8 89 | | | |
| | | | |
| MR 29 '90 | | | |
| | | | |
| MY 6 88 | | | |
| ND 4 '88 | | | |
| | | | |
| MR 22 89 | | | |
| MR 24 '89 | | | |
| | | | |

Yarbrough, Jane.

JC
71
P6 Y37    Plato's The re-
1984       public

# RIVERSIDE CITY COLLEGE
# LIBRARY
### Riverside, California

JE '86

DEMCO